WHAT IS DISPUTE RES

WHAT IS DISPUTE RESOLUTION?

BY

Dr. Peter L. d'Ambrumenil

LLP

LONDON HONG KONG
1998

LLP Reference Publishing
69–77 Paul Street
London EC2A 4LQ
Great Britain

SOUTH EAST ASIA
LLP Asia Limited
Sixth Floor, Hollywood Centre
233 Hollywood Road
Hong Kong

First published in Great Britain 1998

British Library Cataloguing in Publication Data
A catalogue record for this book is
available from the British Library

ISBN 1–85978–834–3

Text set in 10/12pt Plantin by
Mendip Communications Ltd., Frome, Somerset
Printed in Great Britain by
WBC Limited,
Bridgend, Mid-Glamorgan

This book is dedicated to my beloved wife Sarah and my two sons Philip and Frederick who have all as a family supported me during the time I was involved in writing this book.

My thanks are also due to my secretary, Marilyn Francis, whose industrious support made the compilation of this book possible, and our family friend Cilla Grain who carefully proof-read the typescript and whose helpful and constructive comments made this book a realistic possibility.

ABOUT THE AUTHOR

The Author of this book has had a varied and broad-based career.

After a traditional public school education, he spent some year and a half in industry, before entering university to read biochemistry and physiology. Within a short period of time he decided that this was not going to provide a satisfying and interesting career so he chose a university course of greater interest to him. The choice was medicine.

He took a year or so out of the academic life and entered the merchant navy, serving on cruise ships, which were themselves engaged on around-the-world cruising.

Returning from the sea, he entered medical college and thereafter for a period of some years he followed what could only be described as a traditional career. Having undertaken a number of hospital posts he entered general practice, and becoming frustrated with the National Health Service veered towards private practice which in turn led him to become an expert in medical negligence and personal injury. He gained experience in judicial practice.

He gained qualifications in both arbitration and mediation and began to resolve disputes, so gaining much experience in the field of ADR. He went on to set up the company Dispute Resolution Services Ltd., a service company specialising in the provision of personnel competent to resolve disputes in many areas. Since this date his own experience has vastly increased and now he is fully involved in dispute resolution, taking instructions from individuals, insurers and companies.

He has also published a number of articles and books on the subject and lectures widely on the subject.

CONTENTS

TABLE OF ILLUSTRATIONS

The Arbitrator Almoner and Hermit

Three saints by holy fervour fired
To gain the heights of heaven aspired,
But as the well-known proverb says,
Rome can be reached by various ways,
So these by different methods planned
To gain the shores of Canaan's land.
One touched by the expense and care
Which luckless suitors have to bear,
Offered cases to determine
Without a fee, wig or ermine.

Since human laws were first began,
Lawsuits have been the curse of man;
Absorbing half three-fourths or all
Of days which at the best are small.
To cure a state of things so vicious,
Our Umpire thought his plan judicious.
The second of our saints declares
The sick sole object of his cares;
And I praise him: in truth to me
This seems the truest charity.

But sick men troublous then as now,
Our good man vexed enough, I vow.
Capricious, restless, petulant,
Each moment brings a separate want;
And, if no other fault they find,
They cry, "To such and such he's kind:
Spends all his days and nights in caring
For them, and leaves us here despairing."
But these complaints were small to those
Which harassed, every day, the heart
Of him who well intentioned, chose
To act the arbitrator's part.
The plaintiff and defendant, both,
T'adopt his sentences were loth
And swore, with all their might and main,
His partiality was plain.
By such abuse as this disgusted,
The Umpire and Almoner
Each unto his woes entrusted;
And each agreed he could not bear
To be so shamefully mistrusted.
This being so, they sought a glade
Which neither suns nor wind invade,
And there beneath a rugged mountain,

Beside a clear and babbling fountain
They found their friend the Hermit saint;
So each one having made his plaint,
Asked his advice. "Your own pursue,"
Replied their friend; "for who but you
Can make your several wants? To know
One's self makes gods of man below.
And let me ask you, have you found
This knowledge where vast crowds abound?
No; trust me, it can only be
The fruit of sweet tranquillity.
Shake but the water in your vase,
And you no longer see your face;
But let it once more still remain,
And straight your likeness comes again.
'Midst worldly scenes you'll never learn
The love for which we all should yearn.
Believe me friends, the desert's best
For him who'd study his own breast."

To each the Hermit's words seemed good,
And, henceforth, each one sought the wood.

Of course there's always work to do,
Whilst men still sicken and still sue,
For lawyers and for doctors; and
They'll never perish from the land,
Thank mighty Jove, as long as fees
And honours greet their services.
But in such common toils the mind
Can seldom its true likeness find.
Oh you who give your lives away,
And serve the public every day, —
You princes, judges, magistrates,
Exposed to all the angry fates,
Who, when no other ill oppresses,
Are slain by Judas-like caresses —
To yourselves are all unknown;
And if some moment is your own,
For self-reflection, ere it flies
'Tis spoilt by hateful flattery's lies.

This lesson shall conclude these pages;
May it be blessed to future ages!
To Kings I give it, to the wise commend:
How better could my volume end.

With thanks to the Publishers of La Fontaine's Fables, Published by Cassell Petter & Galpin 1856

INTRODUCTION

This book has been written for the lay person who is involved in, or has an interest in, the resolution of disputes. It is hoped that it will also be of interest to many groups of people such as Citizens' Advice Bureaux, trades unions, corporate officers, and professionals in legal and paralegal positions who feel that they wish to enhance their knowledge of the field of dispute resolution.

This book does not deal in great technical depth with legal issues, but aims to provide interested readers with some basic facts which will enable them to understand the system and make a reasoned decision as to which course of action is most appropriate to their particular dispute. By providing the basic facts it will enable them to understand the way in which their legal advisers are handling the case or, if they have no such representative, then it will assist them in understanding the system and the moves made by their opponents.

This book will contain sufficient information for an intelligent layman to understand what is happening and the options which are open to him once he has become embroiled in a legal dispute.

It must be reiterated that it is not the purpose of this book or the author's intention to provide a "do-it-yourself legal service". Despite making this comment it is however possible that in many disputes the matter can be resolved without recourse to a professional legal adviser, and in such cases this book will be an invaluable aid and asset to the party in dispute.

The traditional method of resolving a dispute has always been through the courts and whilst this avenue will remain an important and non-controversial route for pursuing the case, it is inevitable that the recent trends, initiated by Lord Woolf, will mean that the various means of Alternative Dispute Resolution (ADR) techniques are with us to stay.

The range and scope of the methods is wide and the success rate and cost saving is inestimable. Experience from the United States of America, where costs are exorbitant, have shown that the savings made are justification for the methods. In particular they have been embraced by the legal profession which has made the techniques work. Although the income from each case is often less, the increased volume of work adequately compensates for the apparent loss of income.

The better firms of lawyers are already looking at and utilising ADR. Many disputes have been successfully resolved by means of the intervention of alternative methods of resolution.

To those members of the learned profession who oppose ADR, the author can only offer the following advice: read on! You coped with the replacement of the quill pen and even now are generally managing to put the contents of your file cards into your computers. ADR can actually improve your income by resolving disputes, increasing the cash flow and enhancing the image. Only if you are in the position of having just one case have you anything to fear from the implementation of ADR. As indicated above, the term ADR encompasses a range of techniques for the resolution of disputes, some of which are binding on the parties to the dispute—Arbitration—and others which provide for the parties to negotiate—Mediation. The latter category, where there is no finality until there is a binding agreement, falls into this group of techniques. It thus follows that Mediation allows the parties to negotiate and if there is no agreement they are free to go on to litigate or arbitrate the matters not so agreed. More on this later.

Before progressing and despite the fact that the Glossary to this book contains a number of useful definitions, the reader may find it helpful to have a very short explanation of the three most significant terms used within the text of this book.

The first is arbitration, which refers to the resolution of a dispute by a "private judge" whose decision is enforceable through the court system. Mediation refers to a group of techniques whereby one or more independent persons assist the parties to resolve their dispute. Finally, litigation is the term applied to the resolution of disputes through the agency of the courts.

In this context it must remembered that the term "the courts" applies only to those courts with a civil jurisdiction.

This book will help the parties to a dispute understand not only what methods of dispute resolution are available to them but also whom they should approach or appoint with a view to resolving the issues.

CHAPTER 1

DISPUTE? WHAT DISPUTE? WHAT TO DO!

It is a sad fact of life that disputes can and do arise from even the most trivial incidents and activities. They are always totally unexpected and usually highly predictable.

Since man first crawled out of his tree, he has involved his fellow man in disputes, and the history of litigation is well documented in both traditional history and in many venerable holy books with stories of how kings of old dispensed justice to their citizens. Out of this grew the legal systems in existence today. In some cases the implementation of justice was by today's standards severe, and it should not be forgotten that in this country trial by combat was not removed from the statute book until the early 1800s. This removal was precipitated by a case of libel in which the plaintiff (the party commencing a legal action), described as a man of strength, challenged the defendant (the party against whom a legal action is brought), described as a small and weak man, to trial by combat. The method had not been used for several centuries and it came as a surprise to most that it was still on the statute book. However on the statute book it was! The defendant, unable to avoid this form of trial, conceded to the plaintiff, who thus obtained judgment. Very shortly afterwards this particular form of trial was removed from the reach of citizens of the land by a Parliament which had probably not acted with such alacrity for many years.

The thought of being involved in a dispute is so alien to most people that they rarely consider the possibility of one arising until it is too late. Usually the first time the possibility is consciously considered is after the dispute has actually arisen.

This refusal to consider the possibility is the reason why many people avoid purchasing household insurance, and rue that decision only after the burglar has removed their prized possessions or their home has burnt down. It is also the reason why those who drive cars are forced by law to purchase insurance to cover the possibility that they may by their driving kill or injure someone or damage a third party's property.

Similarly it is only once they are embroiled in a dispute that most people wish they had taken out a legal expenses policy. Such policies are not well subscribed to in the United Kingdom, although many people, without realising it, are in fact covered by some form of such insurance. If a dispute does arise, and before clasping one's head and regretting one's lack of foresight, it is worth looking at some sources of such cover. In motoring disputes many policies have as an "add on" legal expenses cover, and many household policies provide at least limited cover in respect of domestic disputes. Similarly those in business may find that membership of their trade organisation has amongst its benefits some level of such cover.

The more forward looking will have gone out and purchased legal expenses cover for both their domestic and business activities. The reader should understand that these broad divisions are often regarded as incompatible by insurers, who will usually only provide one category under the terms of a single policy. The reader should also be certain as to the nature of the cover as many policies contain wide exclusions or require the policy-holder to take out separate cover for different types of dispute. Examples of such grouping will be contract, employment and cover for litigation resulting from the activities of domestic animals. A favourite and often very expensive sphere of dispute is that arising from disputes between neighbours. Many a lawyer makes his fortune on "border disputes" the result of which can be crippling in terms of both finance and emotion for the parties, and it should never be forgotten that such a dispute can make a property unsaleable.

Even the commonest and most innocent activity can give rise to litigation. A shopping expedition gives rise to the purchase of a household item which does not work. You have of course your "statutory rights". There is a possible "breach of contract" which you could pursue through the courts. Likewise if you are injured or your property is damaged there may be a further action in negligence. However the item may injure a visitor to your house and you yourself may be sued for damages. Despite your apparent innocence you may end up paying substantial damages to your visitor.

If you purchase a "package holiday" and the accommodation is far from what you expected, the family have all suffered from "food poisoning" and your holiday was what could only be described as an unmitigated disaster, what recourse to law have you got? This is the time to get out the contract (usually in small print on the reverse of the booking form) and read carefully the terms to which you have agreed. The probability is that there is a clause excluding your right to sue in the courts and binding you to submit the case to arbitration. You then have to ask yourself what arbitration is, and why can you not litigate. A further twist is that whilst you may be entitled to seek legal aid to fund a civil case, there is no such facility to look to the legal aid fund to finance your arbitration costs. It is worth remembering at this juncture that in litigation the winner usually "takes all". The converse is that the loser "loses all". In this respect it means that if you are involved in a legal case and if you win, you may expect to have your costs, less any amounts "taxed down" where appropriate, paid by the loser, but if you yourself should be the loser then you may expect to pay all your own costs together with the costs of the winner. This can result in a massive bill and in more than one case has resulted in the bankruptcy of the loser. The winner may also not be so well off and his own costs may well financially cripple him despite his having "won" the case.

There are of course many other possible instances where the reader may be unwillingly propelled into the legal system. A walk along a road resulting in an accident with a cyclist, with the inevitable injuries to both, may result in a claim by each party against the other and almost certainly neither will have any insurance. The cost of damages for the loser will be high, but the legal costs are likely to exceed any such damages.

In business the possibility and potential for legal conflict is massive. Whether or not one deals directly with the public or only through business intermediaries there is an almost certain probability that at some time there will be a legal dispute involving the business, a third party of the business and one of its own employees. It should never be forgotten that employee disputes are one of the major traumas faced by any business today.

The possibility of a consumer dispute has already been mentioned and such disputes are becoming more frequent, to the extent that they can now be referred to as a fact of life. It does not matter whether the consumer is the purchaser of goods or services, both have been the source of rich pickings for the legal profession.

Under the heading of "contract disputes" it is well worth mentioning actions for debt, as these constitute a major part of the actions commenced by householders and small businesses. Cash flow is a major headache for individuals and the smaller business. England has very few laws to encourage the payment of accounts within a reasonable time, unlike a number of our continental neighbours. Usually the means of encouragement on the Continent is a statutory punitive rate of interest which can be enforced by the courts regardless of whether there was any specific contractual right to such a rate. The rates of interest which may be claimed through the courts in the United Kingdom are restrictive and far from punitive. There is a move currently underway to correct this injustice, but nothing is yet firmly in place.

Thus the first way to protect oneself against the need to commence an action is to ensure that both parties are subject to a contract, which should be in writing and which contains the terms upon which the parties expect to deal. Most disputes between parties seem to arise because there is a failure on the part of one or both to appreciate what it was they actually contracted to do.

Any businessman who is involved in providing services to the public should consult his lawyer or trade organisation to ensure he has a contract which is adequate and comprehensive enough to cover the areas which would otherwise result in a dispute. Particular areas are the cost, the time of payment, and the penalties for late or non-payment. The contract should also have clauses covering the way in which disputes between the parties will be dealt with. Any contract should be regularly reviewed and amended in the light of experience. One very useful clause specifies which court shall have jurisdiction in the case of a dispute. This avoids the plaintiff having the case transferred to the defendant's local court, an action which may cost him dear. Alternatively, and in many ways preferably, a term binding the parties, should any dispute arise, to submit it to arbitration and/or mediation can result in massive cost savings.

When drafting the contract it is essential to remember that there are a number of aspects of legislation which, particularly in consumer disputes, prevent the contracting parties excluding certain rights of the parties pertaining to the deal. Generally the rights of the consumer are protected against the might of the other party.

It is worth highlighting the fact that professional services themselves are a frequent cause of dispute, with allegations of negligence by the client against the professional, and it matters not what the discipline of the professional is: lawyer, estate agent, banker, architect, accountant, surveyor, doctor, dentist or vet. This list is far from exhaustive but provides an indication of the range and scope of those at risk from such action.

It is always difficult to determine what actually causes the plaintiff to start such an action, but common features are that the defendant has failed to provide what the plaintiff believes he or she should have received by way of service. It is not always a failure to provide a proper service, it may just be a perception on the part of the plaintiff that the service has been inadequate.

In order to obtain damages in the law of tort (a group of actions, civil in nature which do not rely upon a breach of contract or a breach of trust), it is necessary to prove the breach and resulting injury and damage. This damage may be any form of injury or damage to property, but in most cases pure economic loss on its own is not actionable in tort.

The other form of action which may be considered is an action for breach of contract. As a general guide damages tend to be less and very much more restricted (but more about this later).

Actions in contract and negligence will cover most but not all the possible causes of action and there are a range of actions in tort which are specific to certain areas of law. Amongst these are dangerous premises, trespass, nuisance, defamation, defective product and a number of others: the reader interested in securing a deeper knowledge should refer himself to any good books on the law of tort and the law of contract.

Another rich area for producing problems is partnership law. Very few people know or understand partnership law and this failure can result in the most severe consequences for those parties involved. The first issue to understand is what a partnership is, and the scope is so wide that the reader who has any doubts as to whether he is a partner should consult a lawyer. Having established that there is a partnership in existence the need for an adequate partnership agreement is paramount and again the reader should consult a lawyer since the failure to do so may result in the default terms of the Partnership Act 1890 applying and in these circumstances the reader may find himself in an untenable situation. He should remember that as a partner he is severally and jointly liable for the actions of his partners, which in practice means he is liable for their debts, including tax liabilities, he is jointly liable for all contracts they enter into, and is jointly liable with them for all their acts of negligence.

In particular in the partnership agreement there should be a very thorough method of resolving disputes between the partners without recourse to law. The cost of litigating such disputes is monumental and inevitably is detrimental to each and every partner. Additionally such disputes inevitably affect the service provided to clients and this in turn raises the chances of a complaint or litigation arising. A clause providing for the resolution of disputes by means of mediation, and if this fails arbitration, will result in massive savings if the partnership is unfortunate enough to fall into internal dispute.

A special area of commerce which will produce much acrimony, expense and emotional distress is the contract of employment. Apart from the fact that the law requires employers to provide employees with such contracts, they should be automatically provided and should detail the employee's duties, rates of pay, holidays, disciplinary procedure and notice. In this way if there is a dispute the contract provides for the means of resolution and hopefully avoids the matter progressing to an industrial tribunal. As before, the best advice that can be given to the employer is to seek assistance from a lawyer and have the contract professionally drafted.

Equally the employee should ensure that such a contract is completed and should ensure that his or her job description and rights are clearly and fully described so that there is no room for later argument.

The field of landlord and tenant is an area which often produces litigation, and for the purposes of this book the issue will be divided into domestic matters and commercial matters.

Domestic tenancies are subject to much legislation and, for this reason if for no other, the landlord contemplating letting property should ensure that he seeks the best professional advice at the outset and that the lease he provides covers all the areas required or made necessary by current law.

Most disputes involving domestic tenants devolve around non-payment of rent and involve actions to recover the rent, the property, or both. The Housing Act 1996 has consolidated and improved the landlord's situation considerably but nonetheless any action involving landlord and tenant can be prolonged and anything that can be done to prevent matters reaching this stage is to be welcomed. If a dispute is not yet finally through the courts then it is possible that mediation might be of assistance to the parties.

Commercial tenancies are a slightly different matter and the author has assisted many parties to such disputes. The causes of dispute are numerous, but the area in which the greatest benefit to the parties can arise from outside intervention is that of imminent insolvency. In such situations the tenant fails to pay his dues and there may be very considerable sums involved.

Later in this book there will be a number of examples as to the ways in which such disputes can be resolved.

No attention is given in this book to family disputes, as these are very well catered for within and around the legal system, and advice can be provided by any lawyer specialising in such matters or by Citizens' Advice Bureaux. This is an area of law where mediation has been utilised very successfully for many years.

If having complied with all the above advice a dispute does arise, derive comfort from the fact that you are not the first and will not be the last person to become embroiled in a dispute with another party.

CHAPTER 2

IN DISPUTE! WHAT TO DO

Having become embroiled in a dispute, and before any action is taken, it is important to identify what the actual problem is, decide if anyone is to blame and, if so, who. The next thing to do is to look at the contract, if any, which covers the particular issue. One should also consider whether there is any particular legislation which, although not detailed in the contract, is relevant to the actual dispute. It is critical if proceeding with any form of litigation or dispute resolution process to be absolutely certain what the actual dispute is about and to be certain of the issues in dispute.

Having considered these points it is then necessary to consider what, if any, action should be taken.

In the first chapter the matter of unpaid accounts was discussed, and it is with this subject in mind that this chapter opens.

Having considered the contract and determined that the sum of money owed is unpaid, it is essential first to ensure that the other party has actually received an account. At the same time you should ensure that there is no obvious reason to justify the other party having refused to make payment. This would include ensuring that no complaint has been received as to the quality or nature of the service or goods supplied.

It is essential that if there is a complaint as to the way in which goods are delivered or services have been supplied the recipient of the product or service should communicate this to the supplier in the shortest possible time. It is no use waiting for the account to arrive and then deciding that a refusal to pay will remedy the situation.

Once it has been concluded that the account is overdue, action is needed to ensure it is paid. At this stage it often pays not to be too aggressive and a letter sent to the debtor requesting payment will more often than not result in the money being delivered. See Appendix 1 for a suitable precedent, "Letter to a debtor whose account is overdue". After a reasonable length of time, and it is suggested that a period of between seven and fourteen days is appropriate, if there is no response from the debtor a second letter should be sent. Again there is a suitable precedent in Appendix 1, "Second letter to debtor". If this second letter fails to produce a result then it is open to the creditor to commence proceedings to recover the debt. Many businesses will at or around this stage invite a debt collection agency to intervene, which will in many cases alienate the customer or client and certainly cost the business money.

Chapter 3 gives a description of the ways in which the court system operates.

If there is an indication from the other party that there is a refusal to pay, it is mandatory to address the issues raised. One should enquire whether there is dissatisfaction with the product or service and, if so, what. Many times a refusal to pay stems from an inability to pay and this needs to be addressed as a separate issue.

Whatever the outcome there is a choice as to how to resolve the problem, and much of the control of choice will lie with the creditor. If it is clear that the debtor is just plain unwilling to pay then the appropriate means of extracting the money will probably be an action through the courts.

If there is a suggestion of an inability to pay, it is often helpful to offer to take stage payments or, if the other party is unwilling to negotiate, it is possible to involve a mediator; more will be said of this later.

Many such problems can be resolved by undertaking adequate credit checks prior to the work being undertaken or goods supplied and preferably before the contract is signed. It is well understood that in the purchase of most consumer goods there is no written contract, but again if the reader is involved as seller in such sales, he will doubtless have credit checking facilities available to him before he allows any credit to the purchaser.

Turning now to other areas of dispute, employment disputes are very well catered for through ACAS and the employment tribunal system, although if a problem does arise there is nothing to prevent either party requesting that the matter be submitted to mediation.

In most professional dealings it is implicit that the person seeking the services of a professional will receive an appropriate standard of advice and where appropriate an adequate standard of care.

Disputes between professionals and their clients are always deeply distressing to the professional and not infrequently seem to engender very powerful emotions in the client. This may well be attributable to the size of fees involved and the potential personal consequences of poor advice. The sooner such disputes are resolved the better: the cost of litigation is inevitably very high, with legal expenses often exceeding the level of any damages awarded.

Complaints are not infrequently justified, at least in part, and the whole argument is prolonged by the wish of professional indemnity insurers not wanting to settle, and indeed by the legal system itself, which often means that such a dispute will continue for years. It is these disputes which cry out for early settlement and they are so often suitable for mediation, which means that a settlement can be achieved where appropriate without the public acrimony which must ensue in the adversarial system utilised in the United Kingdom. Another benefit of mediation in such disputes is the fact that where there is no case for the defendant to answer, this will often be rapidly appreciated by the plaintiff with the resultant withdrawal of the action and inevitable cost savings for both sides.

Partnership disputes warrant further discussion, in that where partners fall out, whatever the reason, the ability of the partnership to service the community decreases, staff leave and in the event of the partnership concluding, the tax and other implications can be disastrous for the partners themselves, irrespective of any culpability.

All partnership deeds should be very carefully drafted and regularly updated. This is the duty of the partnership solicitors and accountants. The deed should address all pertinent matters and issues which lead to disputes. Every trade and profession will have its own specific requirements and the professional advisers to that partnership should be well versed in the needs of their clients. Of critical importance, the deed should provide for a means of resolving any dispute rapidly and equitably, in a manner by which the partners are bound. The ways in which this is achieved vary from case to case and there have been some suggestions earlier in this book, but the deed should include a clause compelling the partners, if they fail to agree a resolution of all or any part of a dispute, that they will submit themselves to mediation. If this should fail to resolve any or all of the issues, then the outstanding issues should be submitted to arbitration. In this way prolonged litigation is avoided and the partnership itself will, hopefully, survive virtually undamaged.

Prevention is the best cure, but, being human, there will inevitably be times when the result of services or the use of goods will give rise to complaints by clients or customers.

All contracts should incorporate adequate enforceable clauses to deal with the dispute after it has arisen.

Adequate insurance should be held by all, which, in the household policy, should incorporate legal expenses insurance, and in this respect one should be sure that the insurers will cover recognised means of ADR, rather than committing the party to litigation. Householders should have insurance to protect them against any damages awarded against them for usual domestic activities, including straying pets, which are a not infrequent source of embarrassment to householders.

All businesses should have a well thought out insurance policy covering both damages awarded against them and the legal expenses incurred in pursuing or defending claims involving third parties. In addition every business should ensure that it is properly advised by its legal and accountancy advisers who should in turn ensure that every business has and uses, where appropriate, well vetted and professionally drafted contracts. In this way the probability of disputes is reduced and, if they do arise, then they can be swiftly and effectively dealt with. Trade organisations can do much to help members in this respect.

The following chapters deal with the three major forms of dispute resolution: litigation, which is resolution through the courts; mediation which is a method which can either be invoked on its own or utilised in the process of litigation or arbitration; and arbitration, which is an alternative to litigation.

CHAPTER 3

LITIGATION

This chapter is devoted to the subject of litigation. It provides the reader with an insight into the subject but does not purport to be a textbook. Any reader wanting greater detail than is provided within this chapter should seek it from a good legal textbook.

If the reader is involved in litigation he will possibly conduct the case himself or more probably seek help and assistance from a lawyer. His first contact with the legal profession will be with a solicitor, who in most cases will conduct the case on behalf of his client. The solicitor may seek to obtain further assistance from a barrister.

The English legal system has developed a system whereby lawyers are split into two distinct groups. There are some areas of interchange but in general terms the first point of contact for the lay (that is non-legally qualified) person is the solicitor. The solicitor will be his or her immediate point of contact with the system and may well be their only legal adviser. He may well act as both their adviser and, if the matter proceeds to court or tribunal, their advocate. However a significant number of solicitors will look to barristers (the other branch of the profession) for specialist advice and advocacy. Any instructions from a solicitor to a barrister are known as a brief.

By this system of "joint professions" the client has available to him or her, in readily available form, high levels of expertise of great significance in specialist areas of law.

Most actions in which the reader may be involved will take place in the county court, although some may be commenced in the High Court. This latter court will deal with disputes over the greater sums of money and cases involving specialist matters such as professional negligence cases. It is important to note that if the case is commenced in the incorrect court, then the case will be transferred to the court with the correct jurisdiction. Inevitably this will result in the cost of such a transfer falling upon the party who has incorrectly issued proceedings.

The legal system is based on an adversarial system, which means that each party who makes an allegation has to prove it and the other side will if it can discredit that evidence. In the time between the issue of proceedings and the trial both sides should and will attempt to reach an agreed settlement. Apart from the savings in costs, the court's time, which is under considerable pressure, is protected. It is a fact of litigation that very few cases commenced actually come to trial.

Before commencing proceedings the plaintiff should send a letter before action to the defendant advising him of the impending action. The letter should contain enough information to enable the defendant to identify the claim and issues against him and should provide him with a reasonable interval, say fourteen days, in which to reply and, if appropriate, settle the claim. An appropriate letter for this purpose appears in Appendix 1.

Having taken the decision to commence an action and decided upon the correct court (see above), it is necessary to decide upon the correct form of action.

First however it is essential to identify the actual defendant or defendants. Although this may seem an obvious comment, it is no use issuing proceedings against an individual if in fact he is an officer of a company, in which case it is the company which should be the defendant. Also, if the person who is to be sued is trading under a trading name, this should be determined at as early a stage as possible. Likewise if the individual is a member of a partnership, is it that individual or the partnership itself which should be the nominated defendant? Further problems arise if the firm or organisation is based in a foreign jurisdiction, and in this respect it should be remembered that both Scotland and Northern Ireland are for the purposes of litigation foreign jurisdictions. It is not impossible to proceed against defendants in foreign jurisdictions but service upon them is governed by special rules of the court of which the prospective plaintiff should make himself aware. The court officers, although not allowed to provide legal advice, are generally exceedingly helpful and willing to give non-contentious advice. They also make it clear that they are unable to state what the outcome of any case will be.

However there is a further and vitally important factor which must be considered before any action can be commenced. This is the time that has elapsed since the cause of the action arose. In law there is a limitation on commencing actions after a specified period of time has elapsed since the cause arose. The actual time varies with the nature of the dispute, being three years for negligence and six years for breach of contract unless the contract was made under seal, when the period is twelve years. The situation is slightly further complicated by the fact that there is an allowance made if the event complained of could not have been known to the party commencing the action within the normal period allowed. In such circumstances the time runs from the time at which the party knew or should have known about the problem.

In the majority of cases, the action will be commenced with the issue of Form N1 (shown on p. 20). Personal injury cases must be commenced using Form N2 (shown on p. 22).

Once the summons has been issued by the plaintiff and served (this is usually effected by the court by means of postal service with a plaint fee being payable by the plaintiff at this time), the defendant will be given a certain number of days in which to serve his defence. If the case involves personal injury, the rules require that a medical report is served with the summons.

It goes without saying that if the reader is the defendant, apart from the letter before action which should have been received by him, the first indication of any action against him may well be receipt of the summons. When the court sends out the summons, it will have sealed it (that is it will carry the court stamp), which means that the document is valid. If there is no such seal it should be presented to the court purporting to issue it for consideration. The issuing court will also endorse on the summons the date on which it will be deemed served, and it is within fourteen days of this date that the defence, if any, must be returned to the court. A failure to do so may result in the plaintiff obtaining judgment by default against the defendant.

The plaintiff will with his summons set out the facts of his claim, in what is known as the Statement of Claim. This document should enable the defendant to identify each and every allegation which is being made against him.

The defendant will have a specified length if time in which to make his reply in the form of a defence, or alternatively to admit all or part of the claim. The document in which he does so is known as the Defence. It is vital to remember that if denying the allegations it

County Court Summons

Case Number *Always quote this*

In the

County Court

The court office is open from 10 am to 4 pm Monday to Friday

(1) Plaintiff's full name address.

(2) Address for sending documents and payments *(if not as above)* Ref/Tel no.

Telephone:

(3) Defendant's full name *(e.g. Mr. Mrs. Miss where known)* and address Company No. *(where known)*

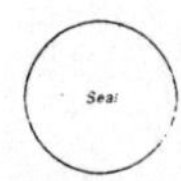

This summons is only valid if sealed by the court. If it is not sealed it should be reported to the court.

Keep this summons. You may need to refer to it

What the plaintiff claims from you

Brief description of type of claim

Particulars of the Plaintiff's claim against you

Amount claimed

Court fee

Solicitor's costs

Total amount

Summons issued on

What to do about this summons

You have 21 days from the date of the postmark to reply to this summons
(A limited company served at its registered office has 16 days to reply)
If this summons was delivered by hand, you have 14 days from the date it was delivered to reply

You can

- **dispute the claim**
- **make a claim against the Plaintiff**
- **admit the claim and costs in full and offer to pay**
- **admit only part of the claim**
- **pay the total amount shown above**

you must read the information on the back of this form. It will tell you more about what to do

Signed
Plaintiff or Plaintiff's solicitor
(or see enclosed particulars of claim)

N1 Default summons (fixed amount) (Order 3, rule 3(2)(b))

If you do nothing	▶ **Judgment may be entered against you without further notice. This will make it difficult for you to get credit.**
If you dispute the claim	▶ Complete the white defence form (N9B) and return it to the court office within the time allowed. The notes on the form explain what you should do.It is not enough to contact the plaintiff by telephone or letter.
If you want to make a claim against the plaintiff (counterclaim)	▶ Complete boxes 5 and 6 on the white defence form (N9B) and return the form to the court office. The notes at box 5 explain what you should do.
If you admit all of the claim and you are asking for time to pay	▶ Fill in the blue admission form (N9A). The notes on the form explain what you should do and where you should send the completed form. You must reply within the time allowed.
If you admit all of the claim and you wish to pay now	▶ **Take or send the money including any interest and costs to the person named at box (2) on the front of the summons.** If there is no address in box (2), send the money to the address in box (1). You should ensure the plaintiff receives the money within the period given for reply.Read How to Pay below.
If you admit only part of the claim	▶ Fill in the white defence form (N9B) saying how much you admit, and why you dispute the balance then **either:** Pay the amount admitted as explained in the box above; **or** If you need time to pay fill in the blue admission form (N9A) and return the forms to the court office within the time allowed.

Costs

In addition to the solicitor's costs for issuing the summons, a plaintiff's solicitor is entitled to add further costs if the court enters judgment against you

Interest on Judgments

If judgment is entered against you and is for £5,000 or more the Plaintiff may be entitled to interest on the total amount.

Registration of Judgments

If the summons results in a judgment against you, your name and address may be entered in the Register of County Court Judgments. **This will make it difficult for you to get credit**. A leaflet giving further information can be obtained from the court.

Further Advice

Court staff cannot give you advice on points of law, but you can get help to complete the reply forms and information about court procedures at **any** county court office or citizens' advice bureau. The address and telephone number of your local court is listed under "Courts" in the phone book. When corresponding with the court, please address forms or letters to the Court Manager. Always quote the whole of the case number which appears at the top right corner on the front of this form; the court is unable to trace your case without it.

How to pay

- **PAYMENT(S) MUST BE MADE to the person named at the address for payment quoting their reference and the court case number.**
- **DO NOT bring or send payments to the court. THEY WILL NOT BE ACCEPTED.**
- You should allow **at least 4** days for your payments to reach the plaintiff or his representative.
- Make sure that you keep records and can account for all payments made. Proof may be required if there is any disagreement. It is not safe to send cash unless you use registered post.
- A leaflet giving further advice about payment can be obtained from the court.
- If you need more information you should contact the plaintiff or his representative.

Certificate of service
To be completed on the court copy only

Served on

By posting on

Officer

Not served on (reasons)

OYEZ The Solicitors' Law Stationery Society Ltd., Oyez House, 7 Spa Road, London SE16 3QQ.

1995 Edition
11.95 CCN1/2

County Court N1

County Court Summons

Case Number	*Always quote this.*	

In the

County Court

The court office is open from 10am to 4pm Monday to Friday

Telephone:

(1) **Plaintiff's full name address**

(2) **Address for sending documents and payments** *(if not as above)* **Ref./Tel. No.**

(3) **Defendant's full name** *(e.g. Mr. Mrs or Miss where known)* **and address Company no.** *(where known)*

Seal

This summons is only valid if sealed by the court.
If it is not sealed it should be reported to the court.

Keep this summons. You may need to refer to it

What the Plaintiff claims from you

Brief description of type of claim

Particulars of the Plaintiff's claim against you

Amount claimed	see particulars
Court fee	
Solicitor's costs	
Total Amount	

Summons issued on

My claim is worth £5,000 or less ☐ over £5,000 ☐

Total claim over £3,000 and/or damages for personal injury claims over£1,000

I would like my case decided by trial ☐ arbitration ☐

Signed
Plaintiff or Plaintiff's solicitor
(or see enclosed "Particulars of claim")

What to do about this summons

You have 21 days from the date of the postmark to reply to this summons
(A limited company served at its registered office has 16 days to reply)
If this summons was delivered by hand, you have 14 days from the date it was delivered to reply

You can

- **dispute the claim**
- **make a claim against the Plaintiff**
- **admit the claim and costs in full and offer to pay**
- **admit only part of the claim**
- **pay the total amount shown above**

You must read the information on the back of the form. It will tell you more about what to do

P.T.O.

N2/1

N2 Default summons (amount not fixed) (Order 3, rule 3(2)(b))

Please read this page: it will help you deal with the summons

If you dispute all or part of the claim

You may be entitled to help with your legal costs. Ask about the legal aid scheme at any county court office, citizens' advice bureau, legal advice centre or firm of solicitors displaying the legal aid sign.

- Say how much you dispute on the enclosed form for defending the claim and return it to the court office within the time allowed. It is not enough to contact the plaintiff by letter or telephone. The court will arrange a hearing and/or will tell you what to do next.

- If you dispute only part of the claim, you should also fill in the part of the form for admitting the claim and either pay the amount admitted to the court or make an offer of payment.

- If the court named on the summons is not your local county court, and/or the court for the area where the reason for the claim arose, you may write to the court named asking for the case to be transferred to the county court of your choice. You must explain your reasons for wanting the transfer. However, if the case is transferred and you later lose the case, you may have to pay more in costs.

How the claim will be dealt with if defended

If the total the plaintiff is claiming is £3,000 or less and/or the claim for damages for personal injury is worth £1,000 or less, it will be dealt with by arbitration (small claims procedure) unless the court decides the case is too difficult to be dealt with in this informal way. Costs and the grounds for setting aside an arbitration award are strictly limited. If the claim is not dealt with by arbitration, costs, including the costs of help from a legal representative, may be allowed.
If the total the plaintiff is claiming is more than £3,000 and/or he or she is claiming more than £1,000 for damages for personal injury, it can still be dealt with by arbitration if you or the Plaintiff asks for it and the court approves. If your claim is dealt with by arbitration in these circumstances, costs may be allowed.

If you want to make a claim against the Plaintiff

This is called a counterclaim
Fill in the part of the enclosed form headed 'Counterclaim'. If your claim is for more than the Plaintiff's claim you may have to pay a fee - the court will let you know. Unless the Plaintiff admits your counterclaim there will usually be a hearing. The court will tell you what to do next.

If you admit owing all the claim

- If the claim is for more than £3,000 and/or includes a claim for damages for personal injury for more than £1,000, you may make a payment into court to compensate the plaintiff (see **Payments into Court** box). The figure of £3,000 includes interest claimed under contract but **excludes** costs and interest claimed under section 69 of the County Courts Act 1984. Send a notice or letter with your payment, saying that it is in satisfaction of the claim. If the plaintiff accepts the amount paid, he is also entitled to payment of his costs.

- **If you need time to pay**, complete the enclosed form of admission and give details of how you propose to pay the Plaintiff. You must reply within the time allowed. If your offer is accepted, the court will send an order telling you how to pay. If it is not accepted, the court will fix a rate of payment based on the details given in your form of admission and the plaintiff's comments. Judgment will be entered and you will be sent an order telling you how and when to pay.

- **If the Plaintiff does not accept the amount paid or offered**, the court will fix a hearing to decide how much you must pay to compensate the Plaintiff. The court will tell you when the hearing, which you should attend, will take place.

If you do nothing
Judgment may be entered against you. This will make it difficult for you to get credit.

General information

Court staff cannot give you advice on points of law, but you can get help to complete the reply forms and information about court procedures at **any** county court office or Citizens Advice Bureau. The address and telephone number of your local court is listed under 'Courts' in the phone book. When corresponding with the court, please address forms or letters to the Court Manager. Always quote the whole of the case number which appears at the top right corner on the front of this form; the court is unable to trace your case without it.

Costs
In addition to the solicitor's costs for issuing the summons, you may have more costs to pay if the court enters judgment against you.

Registration of judgments
If the summons results in a judgment against you, your name and address may be entered in the Register of County Court Judgments. **This will make it difficult for you to get credit.** A leaflet giving further information can be obtained from the court.

Interest on judgments
If judgment is entered against you and is for £5,000 or more the plaintiff may be entitled to interest on the full amount.

Payments into Court

You can pay the court by calling at the court office which is open 10 am to 4 pm Monday to Friday.
You may only pay by:

- cash,
- banker's or giro draft,
- cheque supported by a cheque card,
- cheque (unsupported cheques may be accepted, subject to clearance, if the Court Manager agrees).

Cheques and drafts must be made payable to HM Paymaster General and crossed.
Please bring this form with you.

By post
You may only pay by:

- postal order,
- banker's or giro draft,
- cheque (unsupported cheques may be accepted,
- subject to clearance, if the Court Manager agrees).

The payment must be made out to HM Paymaster General and crossed.
This method of payment is at your own risk and you must:

- pay the postage,
- enclose this form,
- enclose a self addressed envelope so that the court can return this form with a receipt.

The court cannot accept stamps or payments by bank and giro credit transfers.

Note: You should carefully check any future forms from the court to see if payments should be made directly to the Plaintiff.

To be completed on the court copy only
Served on:
By posting on:
Officer:

Not served on (reasons)

"case dismissed on the grounds of insufficient evidence"

is necessary to deny each specific allegation and any allegation not so denied is deemed to be admitted. If part of the claim is admitted this should be stated on the form, and by making payment into court of the admitted sum, costs can be saved. Assuming that there is a full defence or that any partial offer is rejected by the plaintiff, then the matter will proceed.

Upon receiving the Defence, the court will probably issue a set of automatic directions, which is effectively a timetable with which the parties are obliged to comply, with various requirements and with details of when the trial, if it takes place, will occur. Specifically it covers the pleadings, that is the various documents in which the parties describe their stance in the case. Thus it will include the Statement of Claim, Defence, Requests for Further and Better Particulars and similar documents, and discovery, the process whereby each party produces lists of relevant documents which the other party may examine, and if appropriate copy. The idea behind discovery is in part to abolish the old method of litigation affectionately known as "trial by ambush". Other matters which will be dealt with include the nature and number of any experts to be called, and the way in which the parties shall deal with evidence and notify the other party of the witnesses they intend calling at trial.

In personal injury actions the court will restrict medical experts to two and other experts to one.

The reader interested in this aspect of county court procedure should obtain the County Court Rules and refer to Order 17.

In the county court, where a case is to be defended a set of automatic directions will be served upon the parties. The actual terms of the Order will vary slightly between courts but the following is a relatively accurate representation of the type of Order which will be made:

A typical Order 17 rule 11 Order for Directions is reproduced below:

The Court has received a defence in this case which is one to which automatic directions apply.
This means you will not have to come to a court hearing for a District Judge to give directions, that is to tell you what you have to do to prepare your case for trial.
Instead these notes tell you what you must do and the timetable you must follow.
If you want to change any of these directions you must apply to the court.
The timetable begins 14 days after the date given above or 28 days if a counterclaim was filed with the defence.

Step 1 (Both parties)
Make a list of all documents you have ever had which contain information about the dispute between you and the other party. You can do this in the form of a letter or use Form N265 which you can get from the county court. If the defendant has accepted responsibility for the claim, but is disputing the amount of damages you should receive , only documents relating to the amount of damages need be included in your list. Send your letter (or Form N265) to the other party. Tell them where and when they can look at all the documents listed and take copies if they wish. The date you suggest must be within 7 days after they get your list. Alternatively the other party can ask you to send them copies of the documents they want. They must ask for these within 7 days of getting your list. You must send the copies within 7 days of receiving their requests. The other party must repay you any cost involved: e.g. postage, copying charges.
Step 2 (Both parties)
Not later than 10 weeks from the start of timetable.
Agree with the other party when you will exchange copies of written witness statements (including the written reports of any expert witness) you are going to use at the trial. If you don't do this you may not be able to use your witnesses' evidence at trial. All statements should be signed and dated by the witness. You may not have more than two expert witnesses unless the other party or the court agrees.
Step 3 (Both parties)
Any time before trial.
If you are to use photographs or sketch-plans to support your claim you should, if possible, agree with the other party that they are accurate. The person who took the photographs or made the sketch-plan need not be at the trial.
Step 4 (Plaintiff only)
Not later than 6 months from start of timetable.
Write to the court asking that a date be fixed for the trial (unless the court has set a date already). Tell the court how long you think the case will last and how many witnesses you and the other party will have at the trial. The court will tell you when the trial will begin, giving you at least 21 days notice.
Step 5 (Defendant only)
Not later than 14 days before the date fixed for trial.
Write to the plaintiff saying what documents you are going to use at the trial.
Step 6 (Plaintiff only)
Not later than 7 days before the date fixed for trial.
Send the court a bundle of documents both you and the defendant are going to use at the Trial. You should make a numbered list of them, and number each page to correspond with the list. In addition you should send two copies of any of the following (if applicable):
* any witness statements (including expert reports) exchanged under step 2. Say whether they were agreed with the other party;
* any legal aid certificate, if not already filed;
* any request for particulars and the particulars given in reply, and any answer to any interrogatories.

NOTES

1. Personal Injury Claims—In personal injury actions, the steps are varied as follows:

Step 1—Where the injury arises out of a road accident, you need only list the documents relating to the amount of damages.

Step 2 —Each party will be limited to two medical experts and one further expert of any kind unless the parties agree otherwise.

Step 3—In an action involving a road accident, you may use any police accident report at the trial without the policeman who made it having to be there. You should agree the contents with the other party, if possible.

2. Changes to timetable—You and the other party may agree a longer period for steps 1, 2 and 4 but the plaintiff must ask for a date for trial within 15 months from the start of the timetable. If you (the plaintiff) believe you may not be able to request a date within 15 months you must apply to the court and obtain a new timetable.

3. Automatic striking out—If a date for trial has not been requested within 15 months (or 9 months of the date set for requesting a date for trial given in any new timetable) the case will be automatically struck out and you will not be able to proceed with it.

It is available to the defendant to make a payment into court, which is the deposit with the court of the sum of money which the defendant believes it is equitable to pay the plaintiff in full and final settlement of the claim. More will be said of this process in Chapter 6.

Another facet of litigation which should be mentioned is the ability of a party to make a counterclaim. This is the situation in which the defendant in an action, as well as defending or admitting the claim against him, makes a claim against the plaintiff himself. If the value of the claim is small it will be set down for trial as an arbitration. This should not be confused with arbitration in the sense it is used later in this book. It refers to a specific and less formal way of dealing with small claims by the courts, the result hopefully being less expensive and tardy than the full trial.

Whether or not the claim is large or small the trial will involve each side presenting its evidence. Usually the plaintiff commences the case and after he has produced his evidence, the defendant will then produce his. Evidence is taken under oath, and witnesses who are not willing to attend may be compelled to do so by means of a subpoena. More will be said of practice and procedure in Chapter 6.

An action in the High Court is usually commenced by means of a writ. It is necessary to be certain of the correct division of the High Court in which to issue one's proceedings

The procedure in the High Court is far more formal than in the county courts and it is not the purpose of this chapter to advise the

COURT FEES ONLY

Writ of Summons [Unliquidated Demand] (O.6, r.1)

IN THE HIGH COURT OF JUSTICE

19 — —No.

Division

[District Registry]

Between

Plaintiff

AND

Defendant

(1) Insert name.

To the Defendant (1)

(2) Insert address.

of (2)

This Writ of Summons has been issued against you by the above-named Plaintiff in respect of the claim set out on the back.

Within 14 days after the service of this Writ on you, counting the day of service, you must either satisfy the claim or return to the Court Office mentioned below the accompanying **Acknowledgment of Service** stating therein whether you intend to contest these proceedings.

If you fail to satisfy the claim or to return the Acknowledgment within the time stated, or if you return the Acknowledgment without stating therein an intention to contest the proceedings, the Plantiff may proceed with the action and judgment may be entered against you forthwith without further notice.

(3) Complete and delete as necessary.

Issued from the (3) [Central Office] [Chancery Chambers] [Admiralty and Commercial Registry] [District Registry] of the High Court this day of 19

NOTE: This Writ may not be served later than 4 calendar months *(or, if leave is required to effect service out of the jurisdiction, 6 months)* beginning with that date unless renewed by order of the Court.

IMPORTANT

Directions for Acknowledgment of Service are given with the accompanying form.

HCA1/1

The Plaintiff's claim is for

(1) If this Writ was issued out of a District Registry, this indorsement as to place where the action arose should be completed.

(2) Delete as necessary.

(3) Insert name of place.

(4) For phraseology of this indorsement where the Plaintiff sues in person, see Supreme Court Practice, vol. 2, para 1.

(1)[(2)][The cause][One of the causes] of action in respect of which the Plaintiff claim relief in this action arose wholly or in part at (3)
in the district of the District Registry named overleaf.]

(4) **This Writ** was issued by

of

[Agent for]

of

Solicitor for the said Plaintiff whose address (2) [is] [are]

Solicitor's Reference Tel. No:

reader how to deal with such actions. Although the principles of dealing with them are very similar, the way in which matters are dealt with is far more complex and regulated. Almost inevitably anyone involved in such an action will instruct legal advisers to assist them.

Finally a word on funding legal actions in the courts.

Mention was made earlier of legal aid, and if this is available to the party, either plaintiff or defendant, it is a useful and economically sound option which has the benefit of protecting the party against any adverse Order for costs. As can easily be anticipated, such protection is not readily available to the majority of persons. Only the very poor (and, some wags have said, the very rich) will find themselves eligible for such funding.

Legal expenses insurance is available for those who have had the foresight to take it out, or who have the good luck to belong to an organisation which provides such cover automatically.

For those few of the population whose finances are such that the loss of a few hundred thousand pounds is of little significance, think no further, enjoy your litigation and have no worries as to reducing the potential costs. Make a lawyer happy!

For the rest of the population, read on and discover how to keep the costs of litigation down.

"THE MEDIATOR"

CHAPTER 4

MEDIATION

This chapter is devoted to mediation, a process by which many if not most disputes can be settled economically and equitably by the parties through the agency of, usually a single independent third party, the mediator.

This chapter will provide details of what mediation is and how to go about it. It will also give some insight into a number of more sophisticated types of mediation which are more appropriate to commerce than to the individual.

Mediation is a "without prejudice" procedure and therefore allows the parties to put forward suggestions as to how the matter might be settled in ways which they would not be able to do openly. Because of this freedom it is often possible to provide innovative settlements of a type which no court of law or arbitrator could ever provide but by which the parties obtain mutual benefit, and in commerce it often allows them to continue trading, which would never or hardly ever be possible if the case had proceeded through the courts to its judicially imposed conclusion.

Mediation can be invoked from the moment that a dispute arises until the moment before the judge or arbitrator delivers his decision. As a process it is thus very adaptable and capable of fitting most situations.

Mediation was championed in the United States of America, where litigation and the costs of litigation got out of control. Interestingly it is heavily approved of by the legal profession there who have discovered that it settles cases quickly, which means that their fees are rapidly forthcoming. There is a reserve by the legal profession in this country which will not be overcome until it is appreciated that not only the parties but the lawyers as well derive the utmost advantage from the use of the process.

Whilst it involves negotiation it does not follow what most legal advisers consider to be the usual approach to resolving disputes. Mediation is a very specialised form of intervention and there are fewer people who are successful as mediators than there are persons holding themselves out as mediators.

A mediator has no need to be technically competent in the sphere of the dispute, indeed he does not, unlike an arbitrator, have to understand all the issues. It is interesting that the best mediators tend to be people who are capable of lateral thinking and whose personality is such that they can assist parties, sometimes those whose reluctance is notable, to see solutions which would otherwise elude them.

One thing is certain about a mediator and that is that he NEVER imposes a solution upon the parties, unlike an arbitrator or a judge. The essence of mediation is its voluntary nature and the fact that any solution achieved is the result of agreement between the parties themselves. As will be seen later in this chapter, it is this very lack of force that not only makes the process so attractive but also allows the parties to come to resolutions which in a court of law would never be possible and which mean that the detriment which must arise from any dispute is minimised to each and every party to that dispute.

Another facet of mediation which is poorly appreciated is that the mediator is not the agent or advocate of any party to the dispute. He is utterly independent of all parties and will respect the confidences of any party with whom he is dealing. This concept is one which the legal profession has the greatest difficulty understanding, based as it is in an adversarial system. However it is not until this is appreciated and understood that the full benefits of the process will become available to those who could benefit so massively from the use of the process. In fact the idea of mediation, whilst new to the English legal system, has already found a great many eminent proponents amongst the more senior members of the profession and also amongst the more senior members of the business community. There is still a way to go before it is universally accepted by those who have the conduct of disputes, but as insurers and others whose pockets are emptied by the prolonging of disputes come to appreciate its beneficial aspects, there can be no doubt that it will in the very near future become a regular feature of all who have the conduct of such battles.

Mediation has as previously mentioned many forms, and may start from a simple telephone intervention where the mediator, having been approached by one party to a dispute, will make contact with the other party or parties. There is no absolute way in which this contact should be made but the author's own practice is to ensure that the other parties receive a letter in a similar vein to that reproduced below. Naturally, to keep his independence a copy will be sent to the party whose approach has commenced the proceedings.

Dear XXXX
This Company, which specialises in resolving disputes, is an independent Company and is able to provide Mediators and Arbitrators to assist those who are involved in disputes.

We understand that you are currently in dispute with XL. They have approached this Company to see if anything can be done to assist the parties to this dispute come to a resolution of the problems.

I have considered the available documentation and suggest that a suitable means of resolving this dispute would be by mediation. I am taking the liberty of appending some literature on the subject of mediation which I trust that you will find of interest.

Our Mr YZ, who is a qualified Mediator, will be contacting you by telephone within the next few days to discuss whether you feel his services could be of use to you.

The literature appended will vary from company to company but a typical single sheet of information would be as follows:

The frequency of disputes between parties is rapidly increasing and occurs in all fields especially against those in the professions which were previously almost immune from litigation but are now high on the list of those involved. The cost in financial and human terms is difficult to estimate, but the damage to the reputation of the individual and the practice should not be underestimated.

There are several ways of resolving disputes, but it is more important to ensure that a dispute does not occur in the first place.

Litigation is, in this country, an adversarial means of resolving disputes, in which both parties' lawyers try to discredit the other side's evidence and opinions. The final arbiter is the judge who will deliver a decision in accordance with the law and where appropriate the terms of the contract.

Neither side "wins" although one "gets" the "verdict".

The cost in terms of finance and emotion is phenomenal and any business relationship between the parties afterwards is improbable.

In the absence of Legal Aid, the cost may drive the losing party out of business.

It is not the purpose of this article to suggest that ALL disputes should be removed from the field of litigation, but the greater majority of disputes, which in any event usually settle before the stage of trial, are and should remain able to be settled at a much earlier stage by mediation or, in some circumstances, arbitration.

So what are the alternatives and benefits?

Mediation is a means of resolving disputes which is confidential, and in terms of litigation very cheap.

The parties appoint a Mediator, who should be a trained person, who will assist the parties in finding common ground and, where there is such, by exploiting it.

Where there is no common ground the Mediator will facilitate the introduction of suggestions to enable the parties to overcome apparently insurmountable hurdles.

The advantage of mediation is that, being on a "without prejudice" basis, nothing is binding upon the parties until they themselves agree the terms. There is also the advantage that the parties can agree between themselves to "put aside" the terms of a contract and completely renegotiate them on terms to their mutual advantage. This ability to renegotiate a contract retrospectively is something that could never take place in litigation or arbitration. It is however a commercial boon.

The art of the Mediator is to assist the parties to explore such possibilities, enabling them to terminate the matter successfully.

Mediation may be invoked in any dispute from the moment it arises to the moment before a judicial decision is given.

Particularly in professional disputes it is helpful if both parties have obtained any necessary expert evidence and are fully aware of their own position before entering into a mediation.

In simple commercial disputes the opposite tends to be the rule in that the earlier the mediation is invoked the better the result and the greater the benefits to the parties.

In any mediation and regardless of the form or nature of it, it is mandatory for the Mediator to ensure that he deals only with people who have the authority to deal with and settle the matter on account of themselves or their organisation.

One of the problems with mediation is that of persuading the "other side" to go to mediation. Many lawyers still regard the process as a "foreign system" and will discourage its use.

Once a party has made a decision to try mediation it is to their advantage to invite an outside body to make the approach to the other side.

There are various forms of mediation and once the parties have agreed to submit to the procedure these will be discussed with them by the Mediator who will attempt to identify the most efficacious method for their particular problem.

Within days of this letter being sent to the "other party" the mediator will probably make an effort to contact him or her by telephone. He will try to ascertain that he or she is willing to submit to the procedure and that the person he is talking to is authorised to settle the dispute on his party's behalf.

Assuming this is accepted, it is probable that a few telephone calls will be made by the mediator to the parties and having determined the nature of the problem he will then attempt to obtain a settlement.

It is often asked what value of dispute should have resolution attempted by telephone. There is no easy answer and the author would merely submit that the smallest dispute he has settled by means of telephone mediation is £5.00 and the largest is about £500,000. It can be seen from this that there are no hard and fast rules and certainly quantum is a most unsatisfactory identifier. The short answer is that it is always worth a try and if it works then it is the correct method. If further techniques such as the meeting of parties is required then nothing is lost.

A good example of a dispute which at face value would seem highly unlikely to settle under telephone mediation is the following:

Party A asked for the assistance of a mediator in a dispute in which he was involved with another company. It became apparent that the major problem to this party revolved around the non-payment of accounts for heavy engineering plant, already delivered. The type of plant was such that it could only be sold to a specialist market, one in which the party was considered something of an expert.

The debtor party B responded by saying that the machinery did not work and indeed went further, saying that their trade had been damaged by the machinery failures. It soon became apparent to the mediator, however, that the real problem was the financial difficulties that party B were in. The mediator managed to obtain the agreement of party B to pay party A the outstanding sums in a number of instalments. All went well for a few months and then there was a further default by B. A invited the mediator to re-enter the fray. The further investigations made by the mediator revealed the imminent liquidation of B and since it had not yet occurred, the mediator arranged for the transfer of title in the machinery back to A and a licence for A to enter B's premises to dismantle and remove the machinery, all of which was successfully undertaken before B "disappeared".

Following the successful outcome A was very pleased with the process, if somewhat chagrined about his failure to check the other party's credit-worthiness before dealing.

It may be that the party will conclude that the matter is better dealt with on a face-to-face basis and in these circumstances the mediator will seek to arrange a mutually acceptable location for the meeting. It should be a neutral area, that is, not the offices of any party or their representatives, and a usual and very acceptable location is a reasonable hotel in the parties' locality which has conference facilities.

Before any such action is taken the mediator will invite the parties to agree to a contract which lays out the nature of the mediation and the relationship between the parties. A typical example of such a contract appears below.

AGREEMENT TO MEDIATION

1. The following disputes have arisen between the parties [. . .]
2. The Disputants have agreed to request the mediator to accept the appointment as Mediator for the settlement of these disputes.
3. The Disputants have agreed that the Mediator should conduct the mediation in accordance with the attached Guidelines.

This DEED is made on . . . between the Disputants and the Mediator both named below.

IT IS AGREED

1. The Mediator accepts the appointment and agrees to conduct the mediation in accordance with the attached Guidelines for Mediation.
2. The Disputants hereby agree that should any Disputant notify the Mediator that he wishes to terminate the mediation or that the Mediator should decide that a resolution is unlikely, then the said Disputant or the Mediator, as appropriate, shall give notice to the other Disputants, and the Mediator, if appropriate, that the mediation shall be concluded.

The above clause 2 would be the standard clause for a mediation, but reproduced below are two alternative clauses for use in special circumstances, which will be described and discussed later in this book.

2a. The Disputants hereby agree that should any Disputant notify the Mediator that he wishes to terminate the mediation or that the Mediator should decide that a resolution is unlikely, then the said Disputant or Mediator, as appropriate, shall give notice to the other Disputants and Mediator, as appropriate, that the mediation shall be concluded. Upon receipt of such notice the Mediator will advise the [INSERT HERE THE NAME AND STATUS OF SOME INDEPENDENT PERSON SUCH AS THE MANAGING DIRECTOR OF THE COMPANY ARRANGING THE MEDIATION, OR AS AN ALTERNATIVE THE MEDIATOR HIMSELF MAY BE NAMED], who upon receipt of such notice shall appoint an Arbitrator to resolve the dispute. Such appointment shall be accepted by the Disputants as though they themselves had appointed the appointee and further such appointment shall be deemed to have been made under the Arbitration Act 1996, and will be deemed to have been made by the parties to the dispute themselves, in writing.

2b. The Disputants hereby agree that should any Disputant notify the Mediator that he wishes to terminate the mediation or that the Mediator should decide that a resolution is unlikely, then the said Disputant or Mediator, as appropriate, shall give notice to the other Disputants or Mediator, as appropriate, that the mediation be concluded, and upon receipt of such notice the Mediator shall thereby be appointed Arbitrator to resolve matters in accordance with the Arbitration Act 1996. Such appointment shall be accepted by the Disputants as though they themselves had appointed the appointee and further such appointment shall be deemed to have been made under the Arbitration Act 1996, and will be deemed to have been made by the parties to the dispute themselves, in writing.

3. The Disputants bind themselves jointly and severally to pay upon demand the Mediator's fees and disbursements, in accordance with the rates set out in the attached Schedule. The Disputants will between themselves settle all costs of the mediation in accordance with the attached Guidelines.

4. The Disputants agree that they will individually and jointly absolve the Mediator from any liability arising from or in connection with the mediation, and will indemnify him against all claims, demands, costs, damages, proceedings, charges or expenses which may arise in connection with or arising out of the mediation, or the way it was conducted and will not themselves bring any such claim against him (them).

SIGNED AS A DEED AND WITNESSED THIS . . . DAY OF . . .

First Disputant
(Name)
(Signature)
in the presence of
(Name)
(Address)
(Occupation)

Second Disputant
(Name)
(Signature)
in the presence of
(Name)
(Address)
(Occupation)

Mediator
Peter L. d'Ambrumenil
Dispute Resolution Services Ltd.
P.O. Box 106,
Bridgwater TA7 9JE.
(Signature)
in the presence of
(Name)
(Address)
(Occupation)

AGREEMENT TO MEDIATE

APPLICATION No: . . .

SCHEDULE TO THE AGREEMENT TO MEDIATION

The Mediator's Fees

The Mediator will charge at the rate of £. . . per hour, with a Minimum Fee of £. . . .

Time spent by the Mediator will be charged at . . .% of the hourly Fee.

Disbursements

The Mediator will charge at cost any disbursements properly made in respect of:

(a) telephone calls, faxes and other forms of communications;

(b) postage, courier and other delivery charges.

(c) travelling, hotel subsistence and similar expenses;
(d) accommodation and other expenses relating to the venue for the Mediation;
(e) mileage at . . .p per mile;
(f) any taxes such as Value Added Tax which are required to be charged by law will be added to the above and any other charges as appropriate.
The Mediator will be entitled to receive payment for professional fees and all or any disbursements, in advance of incurring them, from any party. The party who pays any such sum to the Mediator will be able to recover an equal share of any such payment from each of the other parties to the dispute as a debt due.

Special Terms

GUIDELINES TO MEDIATION

INTRODUCTION

Mediation is a process whereby a dispute between two or more parties (be they individuals, groups of individuals or companies) is resolved by remitting the dispute to a private hearing before an independent neutral third party (the mediator) whose role is to assist the parties to reach a mutually satisfactory solution to the matters in dispute. The Mediator MAY NOT impose a settlement on the parties.

THE MEDIATOR

Unless otherwise specified, the term "the Mediator" or "Mediator" shall within the context of these Guidelines be read as Dr Peter Lance d'Ambrumenil.

USE OF THE GUIDELINES

Unless otherwise specified by the parties, these Guidelines shall be deemed to be part of the parties' "Agreement to Mediate," although the parties may by agreement vary these Guidelines.

CONFIRMATION OF MEDIATOR

The Mediator shall not embark upon the mediation without the written approval of the parties to the dispute which is to be mediated. Before such approval is given the Mediator shall disclose to the parties any interest he may have in the dispute or with any of the parties, and any other circumstances which are likely to affect the presumption of impartiality.

MEETING OF THE PARTIES WITH THE MEDIATOR

As soon as practicable (and in any event within two weeks) after his appointment, the Mediator will arrange a meeting before him of all the parties to the dispute. The Mediator will fix the date, time and venue of the meeting.

The Mediator may request further details of the facts or issues from any or all of the parties. At least seven days before the meeting, each party to the dispute will provide the Mediator with a brief memorandum setting out the relevant facts and issues in the dispute and their position in relation to these facts and issues. Any documents sent to the Mediator will simultaneously be sent to all the other parties to the dispute by a recognised means. In this case, unless otherwise specified the means will be a recorded delivery letter sent by First Class Letter Post. Prior to the meeting the parties should not send to the Mediator any other documentation, unless at his specific request. No party should attempt to contact the Mediator by telephone and all communications with him should be in writing. Urgent communications may be sent by fax, but as with other communications they should always be copied to the other parties to the dispute, simultaneously.

If necessary, the Mediator may, with the agreement of the parties, visit any place relevant to the dispute, or seek legal or other advice. On any visit the Mediator should be accompanied by a representative of each of the parties.

CONDUCT OF THE MEETING

The parties should bring to the Mediation Meeting all documents and information which they may wish to bring to the attention of the Mediator. It is not appropriate for the parties to bring any witnesses of fact or opinion as the Mediator has no power to hear them and no power to make any decisions concerning such facts.

At the meeting the Mediator may hold joint or individual sessions with the parties and their representatives, and may make suggestions and explore ways by which the dispute(s) may be resolved.

There will be no transcript or record of the proceedings at the meeting. The parties may either represent themselves or if they prefer appoint a suitable person to represent them.

At all times there must be at least one person in each party who is present and who has absolute authority to settle the dispute on behalf of the party he represents.

TERMINATION OF THE MEETING

The Mediator may terminate the mediation at any time if he believes that the matters in dispute between the parties cannot be resolved by mediation. Any party to the dispute may withdraw from the mediation prior to the Mediation Meeting by writing to the Mediator and all other parties to the dispute to that effect, or by withdrawing from the Mediation Meeting.

At the conclusion of the mediation, whether resulting in a settlement or not, the Mediator will return all documents to the parties supplying them, and destroy all his own notes.

CONFIDENTIALITY

The mediation process, including administrative procedures, communications, meetings and private sessions with the Mediator, is a private and confidential process, and no information arising from it shall be disclosed by the parties or the Mediator to any "non-party".

If the mediator has to travel a long distance to the mediation meeting he should be able to arrange his overnight stay conveniently, although he should ensure that his position is not compromised by an inadvertent meeting with any party or their representatives.

This having been said, the author of this book finds that the use of a hotel with good conference facilities is the best choice of venue. There is no necessity for there to be a five star hotel but the premises should be neutral to all the parties, the rooms should be conveniently located for all the parties and there should be easy access, good accommodation and adequate parking. It is essential that the manager is asked to confirm that the rooms are both conveniently sited and soundproof. There is no benefit to be derived from forcing the mediator to make a marathon journey each time he moves between rooms.

The ideal suite of rooms comprises a main room, and one smaller room for the use of each party. If two parties are involved then the room should be capable of taking a horseshoe setup of tables with sufficient room on each limb for all members of a party, with the mediator sitting at the top. If more than two parties are involved the mediator should consider what arrangement of tables would be most appropriate. Once the main meeting is finished and the parties retire to their individual rooms the ideal is a room which has a table and comfortable chairs, one for each member of that party plus at least one spare for the mediator. There should be sufficient coffee or tea in each room and it is important that the parties can have open access to telephones, faxes and catering facilities.

Each room should be near enough for the mediator to migrate between rooms, and far enough to ensure security of discussions from prying ears.

It is interesting that in the weeks and days before the mediation takes place, most disputes will actually settle. The reasons are variable but include the fact that once the mediator is appointed in a commercial case the case will usually devolve upon a more senior officer of the company than previously was conducting the case, and being so much more senior he is able to take a far more mundane perspective of the case, resulting in the probability that it will become much easier to settle.

The author's own experience is that in excess of 75 per cent of cases settle before the actual mediation meeting. This probably proves that it is only when imminent action appears that serious notice is taken of the case, and reflects the fact that in litigation only a very small percentage of cases actually reach the court.

Assuming that the case fails to settle, on the appointed day and at the appointed time the mediator will enter the room to commence the formal part of the mediation. The prudent mediator will allow a few minutes as the parties will already have assembled and this may be the first time they have met and been forced to talk to each other. It would not be the first time that the case had settled at this late stage. After entering, the mediator will sit at the table and open proceedings by introducing himself and inviting everyone else to do so, indicating who amongst them has the authority to settle the matter.

He will reiterate the "without prejudice" status of the proceedings and repeat the implications of this to the parties. He will reassure them of his independence and impartiality and in particular he will note that once the private meetings commence no significance should be placed upon the time he spends with any particular party. He will also reassure them of the absolute confidence which attaches to anything that he is told and his guarantee that nothing will be transmitted to the other side, without that party's express permission. It follows from this that nothing which is directly derived from the mediation is discoverable in the event that the mediation fails and progresses to litigation or arbitration. Nothing which would have been discoverable but for the mediation remains discoverable. It is only documents or other communications which arise in the course of a bona fide attempt to settle the dispute which will be covered by the privilege of "without prejudice".

One other factor which follows from this is that in the event of the mediation being a failure and the dispute progressing to litigation or arbitration, no party to the dispute may call on the mediator to give evidence as to what occurred during the mediation proceedings, including all the preparatory actions and work.

The mediator is likely to remind the parties of their ability to stop the mediation at any point, and depending upon the terms of the Mediation Contract, he will remind them of the consequences of such an interruption. Following this he will invite one of the parties, often the claimant, to address him with the details of the claim. He will strictly time this address and keep the party to within the timetable laid down. Also during a party's address he will ensure that the respectful silence of the other side is kept.

The author has developed the technique of writing down any offer which is to be transmitted to the other side, showing it to the party making it and inviting them to sign it before it is actually transmitted. This avoids any allegation that the wrong terms were actually transmitted—an easy situation to arise when tension is high.

The author usually indicates to parties that where there is a lay claimant, he and not his legal adviser should be given the opportunity to address him. Lawyers find this difficult to manage but the manifest advantages are such that every encouragement should be given to them to allow it. Nothing the party says can affect his or her case as the proceedings are on a "without prejudice" basis and allowing this provides the party's "day in Court" which, if managed well, almost always ensures that there is a greater willingness to settle. After all have told the other side what each thinks of the other, much tension is released. If the lawyers are to address the mediator, it is the author's practice to allow them about two or three minutes. Since the procedure is not an arbitration and since the mediator makes no decisions there is no advantage in apprising him at this stage of the legal niceties. If on the other hand a lay party is making the address, the author allows about twenty minutes. Experience has shown that most lay people given a free hand (mouth), speak for about eleven minutes. If the party is curtailed in his speech he feels further frustrated whereas if he runs out of verbiage he feels he has had his day in court, and justice. It is critical that the mediator keeps the other party quiet during this speech. This is something of an art form and the sign of a well experienced mediator.

Once each party has concluded his or her opening address, the mediator will invite them to withdraw to their respective rooms and it is then that the hard negotiation commences.

By the time the parties are ready to go to their respective rooms the mediator will have achieved a considerable grasp of the dispute and thus will probably invite each party to consider some aspect of the problem in detail whilst awaiting his arrival. This ensures that minds are not idle and provides food for thought. It also occasionally resolves matters, the party having for the first time understood the other party's stance.

In any event the mediator will go to one or other room and in the author's case this tends to be a preliminary visit during which he greets the party personally and ensures he or she is comfortable. In this way he does not spend too much time on the first visit with either party.

Once the mediator is content that the parties are comfortable he will tend to introduce issues and open discussions as to how they may be resolved. If he is skilful and the parties willing it is this that produces the momentum and ends with the resolution.

As time progresses, one party or other may begin to make offers to the other side and the mediator, with the consent of the party, will transmit these to the other party(ies). Almost inevitably counter-offers result and surely but slowly the parties find themselves agreeing a resolution which makes for the end of the dispute.

It needs to be said that once a case is submitted to mediation there is a 90 per cent plus chance of it resolving. In the author's experience, once there is a meeting there has never been a failure to terminate the dispute. The author's experience is wide and considerable numbers of cases have been dealt with. However even he does not expect his records to remain unbroken for ever. However, that having been said, it provides a very good indicator that the process works, and works well.

Some examples of mediation

It will be of help to the reader to appreciate how mediation has helped in specific cases and thus a few examples will be provided. Before relating them the author would make the point that one of the major successes of mediation is to cause a party whose case is a "lost cause" to withdraw. That is not to say that this applies to many cases but it is certainly relevant to the small number of cases, which whilst pursued in good faith are clearly "non starters".

In a dispute between neighbours over rights of way, solicitors acting for both had indicated the cost of legal action would be high and the outcome far from certain. Party A claimed a right of way down a lane, Party B denied there was such a right of way. It was contended by B that there was a limited right of access but that A's contention that there was a vehicular right of way was wrong. Legal costs were mounting and one party was advised that the probability was that if they continued they would receive an injunction and an adverse bill of costs.

The mediator helped the parties agree that B would grant an unconditional right of way to A, assuming that they had the right to do so, which on the facts seemed improbable. A agreed to cease certain provocative actions towards B, which were for a greater part the causes of the whole action. The dispute was resolved and both parties' legal advisers commended it to their respective clients.

The legal advisers drafted the Deed of Agreement and all parties went away content.

It should be noted that the presence of good independent legal advice did much to help the resolution and one of the best bits of advice that can be given to people who want a dispute mediated is that they should, unless they are legally competent, consider ensuring that they have a legal adviser present. His importance will become obvious when any agreement is being drafted and for the lay person against a large commercial concern it is one of the ways in which his interests can be protected.

It should be noted that the mediator is NOT there to protect the interests of any individual party, he is there to achieve a resolution of the dispute.

In another case the way in which lateral thinking can enhance a resolution is adequately demonstrated.

One party to the dispute was an insurance company and the other was a motorist whose car had been involved in an accident through no fault of his own. The insurance company represented the other driver whose guilt was not disputed. The major problem was that the driver valued his claim at more than the insurer was prepared to pay. There was a gap of about £2,000.

During the mediation the insurer increased its offer to reduce the deficit to about £1,000. There was however no agreement and it seemed that the whole dispute would proceed to court.

The mediator decided to run an idea past the insurer which was that the insurer should offer the driver a year's free insurance. Initially the claims manager was taken aback and somewhat sceptical; however he agreed subject to suitability.

The driver, who had an 18 year accident-free record on exotic cars, agreed subject to the insurer recognising his "no claims bonus".

The mediator returned to the insurer and terms were agreed, it being pointed out to the insurer that if he accepted the proposition and the driver was claim-free he faced little or no cost, and on the basis of track record it seemed probable that there would be no further accidents, the driver being free of culpability in this last incident. It was further pointed out that if the driver was content with the service from the insurer he would probably renew with him, ensuring a premium income for a number of future years—drivers not readily changing their insurer.

Both parties were exceedingly content with the resolution and the mediator was much pleased.

This case shows the versatility of the system and the way in which it can resolve problems in a manner which could never be achieved through a court but which are blessed with the complete agreement of all concerned. The cost saving is huge.

A further dispute which demonstrates how mediation can assist parties is one which the author was involved in as mediator. He has changed all identities to ensure anonymity for the parties.

The dispute was a partnership dispute involving professional people and the results of the dispute were damaging their professional practice. After several years of costly dispute and several months of litigation, their legal advisers, who were only too aware of the costs of litigation in the Court of Chancery and the personal damage that could ensue, recommended mediation to their respective clients. There were three parties and seven partners—a mix of husbands and wives—and all they could agree upon was 39 heads of dispute and, of course, the name of the mediator.

The mediator was faced with a professional nightmare.

It was decided that the parties wanted a medarb agreement, that was if there was no resolution they wanted the matter resolved by arbitration.

The mediator decided that since the partnership deed was clearly at least part of the problem, much would be resolved if this obstacle could be overcome. He therefore suggested to all those present at the opening meeting that before proceeding, they might benefit from agreeing at this juncture to set the partnership deed aside. Surprisingly they did.

One by one the different issues were resolved and equitable solutions inserted. Finally there was only one issue and this appeared likely to be the sticking point until the mediator announced that he would give 20 minutes before declaring the mediation a failure and submitting the whole matter to arbitration.

Legal advisers to the parties drew their attention to the fact that if the matter went to arbitration they would lose the negotiated deals to be substituted by the arbitrator's decisions, there would be substantial added costs and the partners would universally lose as they had in the mediation achieved terms which were substantially better than could ever be obtained in litigation.

The result was that the final point was agreed and the whole dispute started to unravel.

It was yet again the lawyers who then had to work as they redrafted a new partnership deed, a work which took several weeks. In order to bring finality the parties invited the mediator to provide an Arbitral Consent Award on the agreed terms, which ensured the compliance of all. (See Chapter 7 for details of a consent award.)

The significance of these comments will become apparent in Chapters 6 and 7.

It will be noticed that the Mediation Contract provides for immunity of the mediator against any action by any or all of the parties. This is important in ensuring the proceedings can take place in an atmosphere free from any adverse pressure or threat.

The costs of the mediation are in principle equally shared between the parties. In practice it is possible that the costs will themselves become a part of the settlement of the dispute with one or other party agreeing to underwrite the whole or a major part. This is almost invariably the case when one party is an individual and the other a major commercial concern. The important thing is that the agreement is not reached until the mediation has commenced and thereby the mediator's independence is protected.

Where the parties are involved in a dispute which arises from a contract which incorporates its own dispute resolution procedure, they should ensure that there is a complete agreement between themselves to vary the terms if this is what is to happen, should mediation be invoked.

Tribunal mediation

It has been mentioned that there are many forms of mediation, and not all can be discussed within the constraints of this book which is designed for the readership outlined in the Introduction. However, despite this, mention will be made of tribunal mediation.

This form of mediation is particularly applicable to commercial concerns. Although not universally, it is frequently the fact that disputes in commerce are handled by middle grade managers. In most cases this is a perfectly acceptable way of dealing with disputes and most terminate at that level. However, occasionally a dispute arises in which the middle grade officers are not technically proficient enough or are unwilling to expose their own inadequacies by bringing a particular issue to the attention of a senior manager.

It has already been mentioned that once a senior officer is involved there is a tendency for disputes to terminate rapidly. Sometimes, however, there is a real difficulty which is not easily overcome. In these circumstances tribunal mediation may be the answer.

It works by each party appointing a senior manager, who should be a genuinely very senior officer of the company and also senior to the manager currently with the conduct of the case. At the same time as these arrangements are made, an independent mediator is appointed who then sits with the two, or more if more than two companies are involved, and this tribunal is addressed by both or all managers who previously had the conduct of the case.

Experience shows that the more senior men are fully conversant with the technical aspects of their trade or profession and, with the assistance of the mediator, it is rare for the whole dispute not to be concluded within a very short time.

The use of such a tribunal mediation is exceedingly rare in the United Kingdom, but is far from rare in the United States of America. Indubitably, as its advantages become apparent to those in authority, this means of resolving disputes with its massive savings in costs will become a more frequently utilised method of resolving disputes in the business community in this country.

CHAPTER 5

MEDARB

This chapter is a short one and discusses the subject of medarb. Many English lawyers will say that it has no place in the resolution of disputes but experience from the United States of America provides much evidence to the contrary and indeed the author's own experience is that if used judiciously it can expedite the settlement of disputes.

In order to understand what medarb is, it is necessary to have a basic understanding of the way in which it developed.

Mediation, as is patently clear from the earlier chapters, is a voluntary non-binding form of dispute resolution. That is until the dispute is resolved and agreed, at which time the agreement becomes binding upon all the parties involved (see Chapter 7).

In some disputes the parties require that there is a final and certain outcome but that this is attended by a certain versatility in the resolution. It is for these people that medarb was designed and for whom it will be of the utmost service.

As with mediation there are variations in the way in which the topic is presented and utilised, although far fewer than with mediation itself. As with mediation the parties can discuss the issues involved and produce innovative resolutions to the extent that they are able, as can any person utilising mediation. However if they then become stuck and reach a stage at which they are unable to agree any more, they still have the assurance that the matter will not continue along an expensive and acrimonious track of prolonged litigation because once the matter sticks irrevocably the whole dispute becomes subject to arbitration, which must result in a certain and determinate outcome.

The reader is referred to the Contract for mediation in Chapter 4 which incorporates a number of clauses, and reference is made to alternative clauses 2a and 2b. The significance of these is obvious upon reading. What may not be so obvious to the lay reader is the significance of the mediator being appointed as arbitrator. It is this that provides the contention for English lawyers.

The mediator, having been privy to the most intimate dealings of the parties and having become aware of each party's strengths and weaknesses, is then expected to act judicially and put out of his mind all that he has learned. Even if he can, the beliefs of the parties themselves may be somewhat stretched. Despite all this the author has on a number of occasions accepted the post of arbitrator after acting as mediator and the results have yet to be challenged or criticised by the parties. It must however be stated that the mediator acting as arbitrator has many disadvantages and cannot be recommended to the majority of disputants.

A far preferable option is for the mediator to appoint an independent party to act as arbitrator. This avoids providing the parties with further grounds for dispute over the identity of the arbitrator.

One very powerful argument for the mediator acting as arbitrator is that in a few disputes in which he has acted, the parties have resolutely refused to come to a complete agreement until it has been pointed out that he will terminate the mediation and invoke the arbitration clause. Without exception on each and every occasion this has been effected, the recalcitrant party has immediately agreed the outstanding issues, knowing that the outcome of an arbitration must by definition be less favourable than the options available under the mediated settlement.

The whole issue is, however, not without its difficulties and if the mediator intends to act as arbitrator he should not rely upon the original appointment but should ensure that all parties reconsider the situation and if they are content then they should formally appoint him, in writing, disregarding the original Deed of Appointment. In this way the likelihood of a challenge to the integrity and independence of the arbitrator is much diminished.

Where the mediator appoints the arbitrator who is to deal with the dispute, the parties have the benefit of certainty. The nomination of the arbitrator having been resolved without itself having become the object of a separate dispute between the parties, and the inevitability that such an appointment means that the dispute will resolve, come what may, has many advantages. There is, however, a down side and this is that if the mediation fails, then there is also the inevitability of further expense for the parties before the matter is concluded. It should however be remembered that mediation will conclude finally not less than 90–92 per cent of all disputes submitted to the process.

One further process which will be mentioned under medarb, although it is not truly medarb, is that of expert determination.

Expert determination is used in a limited number of spheres in the United Kingdom. It is a process whereby the parties jointly appoint an expert in the field of the dispute, thus it is only appropriate where there is in fact a technical issue to be determined. The expert should investigate the issues and will inevitably come to take a view on the facts he determines. Once his investigation is complete he will report to the parties and provide them with his opinion. His opinion is not binding upon the parties, unless there is a prior agreement to that effect. Being an expert appointed by all the parties it is hoped that his opinion will be at least persuasive. In most cases this action and report will result in the resolution of the dispute, but if it does not then in any later litigation, or arbitration, that expert's opinion can be called by the parties. This is a major difference from the position of a mediator who, once the mediation is concluded, cannot be called by any party to the dispute who is later involved in any proceedings.

It can be seen from this chapter that mediation has much to offer litigants and is capable of saving them a very large percentage of costs. It is adaptable enough to be utilised at any stage in the dispute from the moment the dispute arises, and before any litigation has been instigated through to the moment before the judge delivers his decision or the arbitrator publishes his award.

CHAPTER 6

ARBITRATION

This chapter is devoted to arbitration, a procedure by which disputes are conclusively terminated in a judicial manner, by an arbitrator, who is recognised by law as such and whose decision the courts will enforce as a judgment of the court.

The term arbitration is much misused and has a number of meanings within the common usage.

Arbitration is a very old protocol and highly respected in commerce, where it is the way in which disputes are resolved without the massive costs of litigation. The degree of formality is governed by the wishes of the parties and this is what makes the process so attractive. The interested reader should look up the various specialist types of arbitration, such as "look sniff" arbitrations utilised in specialist London trade arbitrations.

Since man has traded he has wanted a means of resolving his disputes with fellow traders and it is in this way that arbitrations arose. Usually a well-respected wise man was appointed and his decision was accepted as binding upon all concerned. The principle is little different today.

The term arbitration is applied to a number of procedures which have nothing to do with the term and method of arbitration used within the meaning of this book. The county courts have a system of arbitration, which although it is similar in principle is conducted by appointed judges and conducted under the rules of the court.

Arbitration is also the term used in employment disputes when the organisation ACAS is involved in attempting to resolve the matter. Again this is no relative of arbitration as described in this book and undertaken under the auspices of the Arbitration Act 1996.

In this book the term arbitration is applied to the process whereby parties to a dispute appoint a "private judge" to determine the evidence and issue an award which is recognised by and enforceable through the courts.

Although it is necessary to make reference to specific parts of legislation it is hoped that the reader with no legal knowledge will not find this too daunting. It follows from this that the procedure is important and like mediation there are a number of types of arbitration. This chapter will deal with just two types, the documents-only arbitration and the full arbitration including a hearing.

The first and most important feature of arbitration is that the parties to the arbitration must agree to submit themselves to the procedure. This decision can be made after the dispute has arisen, in which case the parties are left with having to decide upon and appoint a suitable person. Or there is the situation which probably more commonly arises when the parties are in contract and the contract incorporates a term whereby, in the event of a seemingly insoluble dispute between them, they should submit the dispute to arbitration. Most clauses also define the way in which the arbitrator will be appointed and by whom.

If such an arbitration clause is in existence the parties should appreciate that the courts will enforce it and not leave a party the right to litigate, any such action being "struck out" pending the outcome of the arbitration. There is an interesting ramification from this, which is that whilst legal aid is available for litigation, to those who are eligible, no such availability of legal aid exists for pursuing an arbitration. It thus follows that the impecunious person, who could, but for the arbitration clause, pursue the matter through the courts, is barred from doing so. Additionally his position is compromised by an inability to fund the action. Whether this is justice or not is a matter of debate, but it can be properly argued that the arbitration clause is part of a contract voluntarily entered into by competent adults and thus there can be no argument that the party is bound by the arbitrator's decision. This may seem somewhat unfair in the light of today's modern tendency to provide contracts referring to terms held elsewhere, or buried in the small print, but such is law!

In order to assist the reader, there are two documents contained in the Appendices to this book. Appendix 2 is the Arbitration Act 1996, referred to previously and being the current legislation governing arbitrations within England and Wales. The Act was passed to increase the powers of arbitrators and so make them more independent of the courts. It also enhanced the arbitral procedures within the jurisdiction of England and Wales, enhancing its international reputation as a centre for international arbitration.

The second document is the UNCITRAL Model Rules for Arbitration which appear in Appendix 3 to this book and are reproduced to demonstrate a very comprehensive basic set of rules. However, they do not contain many of the powers available under the Arbitration Act 1996. It should be noted that they are not, however, the only set of rules. Nearly every trade organisation of note and body dealing with disputes will have its own set, some more and some less comprehensive.

So the next question is "Am I committed to arbitration?". To answer this one needs first to look at the contract and see if there is a clause binding one to go to arbitration in the event of a dispute arising. It also follows that in order for there to be a commitment to arbitration there must be a dispute. This may seem obvious but does require stating. If there is no such clause then it may still be open to the parties to go to arbitration to resolve the dispute. In order to do this the consent of both parties is required. One party cannot, in the absence of a pre-existing contractual requirement to do so, force another party down the track of arbitration.

If one party has already commenced litigation then the other party to such a contract can apply to the court to have the action stayed pending the outcome of the arbitration. This aspect of the procedure has been discussed earlier in this chapter and the pertinent comments are there and will not be repeated.

Having agreed, willingly or otherwise, to submit the dispute to arbitration, the next move is to find an appropriate arbitrator. The contract, if any, may provide for the appointment of an arbitrator by a specific person or authority, for example the president for the time being of the Royal College of Surgeons. The actual officer or organisation does not matter and it may be someone as easy to contact as the partnership accountant. If such a person is named then look no further. Having advised the person or body of the fact that there is a dispute, he will nominate an arbitrator and the parties will have no choice.

If the arbitrator is appointed by a third party he will write accordingly to the parties, but if the parties themselves are to appoint a mutually acceptable arbitrator, then they should approach him and he will signify to them whether he is prepared to accept the appointment. Assuming that he is and that his terms are acceptable to the parties, they should appoint him by means of a written document. A typical document appointing an arbitrator is reproduced below:

Whereas disputes have arisen between us, in relation to [*insert here a brief detail of the disputes*], we jointly appoint Dr Peter Lance d'Ambrumenil to act as Arbitrator, under the terms of [*insert here the rules under which the arbitration is to be conducted or in default, "The Arbitration Act 1996"*].
Signed .... Signed ....
Dated ....

The arbitrator upon receiving this document will reply in writing accepting the appointment.

Once the appointment has been accepted, the arbitrator is in a position to proceed. It will probably be obvious to the arbitrator at this stage whether the dispute should be dealt with on the basis of documents only or whether he believes the matter should proceed to a full hearing. The wishes of the parties are of course highly relevant and even if the arbitrator and one party decide the matter should be resolved by means of a "documents only" arbitration, the remaining party has the right to ask for a full hearing. Any party making such a request should bear in mind the tremendous difference in costs which will arise if the matter goes to a hearing, and if it is considered that the hearing is not essential the arbitrator can make appropriate orders for costs so that it may be prudent to consider the most efficient means by which the dispute can be resolved as well as the most glamorous.

Assuming that there is no obvious reason to hold a hearing and the parties themselves have agreed, the arbitrator will probably issue an Order for Directions providing for the claimant to deliver his statement of case, which should include not only the facts of the claim but any supporting evidence such as statements of witnesses, invoices, receipts, photographs, plans or other documents which the party wishes to have considered and which the arbitrator will find useful in judging the facts. All documents submitted should be carefully placed in a folder, preferably numbered, and should be in a logical order. A duplicate of this file should be sent to the other party, the respondent.

A typical Order for Directions is reproduced below:

IN THE MATTER OF THE ARBITRATION ACT 1996
AND IN THE MATTER OF AN ARBITRATION BETWEEN
.... Claimant
and
.... Respondent

Upon receiving submissions from both the Claimant and Respondent
I DIRECT THAT:
The Parties shall communicate with the Arbitrator only in writing and any such communication shall be served simultaneously upon all other parties to this Arbitration. All documents served by one party upon the other shall be served either personally or by means of First Class Letter Post, in which case they shall also be delivered under the Recorded Delivery service. Service shall be effective if made at the address registered as that of the party, when appointing me as Arbitrator. A communication sent by Recorded Delivery First Class Letter Post shall be deemed served twenty-four hours after it was posted unless such shall fall upon a weekend or public holiday in which case the letter will be deemed served the day following such weekend or public holiday.
The Claimant shall, within 28 days of the date of this Order, deliver his Statement of Case to the Respondent, with a copy to me.
Within 14 days of effective service of the Claimant's Statement of Case, the Respondent shall deliver his Statement of Case to the Claimant, with a copy to me.
There shall be a further period of 14 days after effective service of the Respondent's Statement of Case during which the parties may submit observations on the other's case. Any such observations shall be made in writing and be served upon the other party with a copy to me.
Once this period of time has elapsed I shall consider the evidence and in due time publish my Award.
Liberty to either party to apply
Signed Arbitrator dated......................
This Order will be sent to each of the parties or if they have representatives it will be sent to them instead.

The arbitrator will probably have given the party about seven to fourteen days to prepare and deliver his bundle, but this will depend upon the facts of the case. There will be a similar time allowed to the respondent to submit his statement of case. As can be seen from the draft Order the arbitrator will allow a further short period of time before he adjudicates the matter for the claimant to make any further comments upon the respondent's submissions. Naturally such observations must be restricted to the actual submissions and it is not permissible for the party to bring new facts or issues into the arbitration at this stage. If it is clear that further facts need to be considered then an application should be made to the arbitrator for permission to amend the statement of case.

If such permission is granted the arbitrator will then again allow time for the other party to make any observations upon this further evidence that may be considered appropriate.

Once this evidence has been submitted the arbitrator will make his award. The form of the award is not fixed, but a typical form of award is reproduced later in this chapter.

It will be noted that the award provides details of the claim and the arbitrator's reasoning and conclusions. This is known as a reasoned award and is the type of award which can be expected in most arbitrations. Only if both parties agree that they do not want a reasoned award will the arbitrator not produce one. The grounds for requiring such a non-reasoned award are slim and it would be most unusual and indeed even most unwise to request one, since to do so would make any appeal more difficult and there is no real saving in costs to be made by restricting the arbitrator's duties to providing just a decision.

If the case is to be dealt with by means of a more formal procedure including a hearing, the process will take much longer and there will be far more involved for both the parties and the arbitrator. The probability is that some parties at least will feel the need to be represented by professional advisers and so therefore the cost will escalate.

Assuming that there is to be this fuller procedure, the way in which the process will be controlled will be within the gift of the arbitrator who, acting within the rules upon which the parties have decided, will conduct the process judicially. Naturally it is possible to be as formal or informal as the parties require, providing that the rules are complied with and the rules of natural justice are observed.

There follows a description of a typical arbitration with an explanation of its various phases. The reader should always bear in mind that no particular details are binding upon the parties or the arbitrator. The fulfilment of compliance with any rules and natural justice are, however, of paramount importance.

Having been approached by the parties or appointed by an appropriate authority, the arbitrator will consider whether he has the appropriate skills and knowledge to undertake the task of acting as arbitrator and then he will consider whether there is any reason why he should not do so. Examples of possible reasons would be a personal or business relationship with one of the parties, or a professional knowledge of the dispute itself, that is a previous involvement with the facts of the matter.

Assuming that no such bar exists the arbitrator will then formally accept his position, having previously apprised the parties of his proposed fee structures and obtained their agreement to such. This is important because there is a contractual relationship between the parties and the arbitrator and as such the terms of that contract are made at the point of acceptance by the arbitrator of the party's offer. Thereafter it is not possible, without the unanimous consent of the parties, to alter the terms of the contract and thus there is no ability to insert details of the fees to be charged at a later stage.

A number of arbitrators will utilise the time of acceptance to include a notice to the various parties which provide informal but no less essential instructions, including such important restrictions as the need for each party to ensure that they never telephone the arbitrator and that all communications to him are made in writing and simultaneously copied to all other parties to the arbitration. This is good practice as it prevents any inadvertent communications with the arbitrator which might jeopardise his independence, in which circumstances he would have to stand down and the parties would inevitably be faced with additional expenses, which later in the proceedings could be massive, if a new arbitrator had to be appointed.

Once it is established that all is in order, the arbitrator may well decide that a preliminary meeting was necessary. This meeting can be crucial in determining how the arbitration will be conducted and will also be the time when the arbitrator endorses the whole proceedings with his judicial style. The meeting should be attended by at least one representative from each party and this may be the claimant or respondent in person or their representative. At an arbitration there is no requirement for representatives to be instructed, and even if they are there is no need for them to be qualified legal advisers.

The arbitrator in considering where such a meeting will be held would be prudent to consider the wishes of the parties in respect of date, time and venue.

The meeting will be convened and it is at this meeting that the parties will have a formal opportunity to challenge the jurisdiction of the arbitrator if they have not already done so. It is unlikely that this will arise if the parties have themselves appointed the arbitrator.

Other issues which need to be dealt with will include the arbitrator's need to be satisfied that his appointment is valid, and whether there are any doubts or challenges to his jurisdiction. This latter word refers to the areas which the arbitrator is authorised to consider as part of his judicial activities. Again this is probably not going to be at issue, but if it is, this meeting is the time at which such objections should be raised.

Once these fundamental matters are out of the way, the more mundane but no less essential matters will be discussed.

The arbitrator will want to know if either party is to be represented and if so by whom; specifically he will want to know if counsel (a barrister) is to be instructed. Then will follow the pleadings. The pleadings are the documents by which the parties notify the other party or parties and the arbitrator of the details of their case.

The claimant (the person or body instigating the claim) will have to serve (the word for delivering a document to the other party) his Points of Claim, and the time in which this has to be delivered will be decided by the arbitrator and his decision will be influenced by the complexity of the matter. Once this document has been served the respondent will have to reply with a Points of Defence. Again there will be a specified time schedule for the delivery of this document. If, after the service of these documents, there are points which are not clear to them they are able to serve Requests for Further and Better Particulars, to which the other party must issue a formal Reply.

The pleadings will contain the facts upon which the parties' cases are built but not the law supporting them. Neither will they contain the statements of the various witnesses which the parties intend to call (compare this with the Statement of Case in a documents only arbitration). Following the completion of these documents (the close of pleadings), there will follow a sequence of processes all directed by the arbitrator.

Discovery of documents will take place, with each party providing for the other lists of those documents in their possession and control or previously in their possession and control, which are pertinent to the case. Some documents may be in existence which are privileged.

The notion of privilege is a complex one and outside the scope of this book, but suffice it to say that amongst such documents are communications between a lawyer and his client. The list is fairly long and some documents may be subject to privilege in certain circumstances but not in others. If a party believes that any such document which they possess falls into this category then they should seek advice from a competent professional adviser. If all else fails the arbitrator can be invited to make a ruling upon the standing of any particular document.

Once the lists have been served by each side a short period of, say, seven to fourteen days will be allowed after which there will be an entitlement to inspect the declared documents held by the other side. There is also an entitlement to copy them. In most cases, with a little co-operation between the parties, copies can be sent automatically, assuming that the list is not that long, which in most relatively simple disputes it will not be.

At some time after this there will be a mutual exchange of expert witness reports and then witness statements.

It is most helpful to the arbitrator if the parties, when discussing witnesses, can provide details of any witnesses who may require unusual facilities for the taking of oaths. More will be said of this later.

The arbitrator will at the preliminary meeting address the subject of expert witnesses and decide with the parties if they are necessary and, if so, how many will be permitted on each side. Generally if one party is allowed such a witness the other party will be permitted to "match that witness" with a similar one of his own. Such expert witnesses are senior members of their profession or trade whose opinion as to the way in which their discipline within that profession or trade functions is well respected. Such witnesses should restrict their evidence to their own specific sphere of expertise and, no matter whose side instructs them to prepare the report, their opinion should be strictly their own. There is nothing to be gained by writing the report and providing an opinion which is acceptable to the client if this is not in accord with what is truly accepted by the profession. A minority view is completely acceptable if it is a respected minority view. Such witnesses should remember that they will be cross-examined upon their report and if they are not able to support it under oath their credibility is damaged and their client's case is destroyed. It is better to be wholly truthful early on, even if this means that one's client's case fails at a very early stage.

The appearance and presentation of the expert witness is crucial and a favourable image will inevitably impress the arbitrator.

Of no use to the arbitration or the client is the claimant's expert who reliably "trots out" just what the client wants to hear. Equally so the respondent's expert. The professional reputation of the rogue expert is soon destroyed.

It is highly probable that if there are expert witnesses involved in the hearing, the arbitrator will order that there should be a "without prejudice" meeting of those experts, at some time after the exchange of their reports and the witness statements. The purpose of such a meeting is to narrow the issues between the experts and in most if not all cases such a meeting will result in the experts agreeing the case on the various sets of facts available. If this happens, their own

"The Expert Witness"

attendance at any hearing becomes unnecessary and the cost saving in time and professional fees is often very considerable.

At the time of the preliminary meeting the arbitrator may consider applications by the respondent for an Order for Security for Costs against the claimant. There are a number of grounds on which such an Order may be based, but if the claimant is known to be impecunious the respondents may well apply for such an Order to protect their own position if they win the case.

Any Order for Security for Costs is governed by the terms of the Arbitration Act, unless rules in force also cover the situation. In either case the arbitrator must act judicially in making such an Order and it is not one to be made lightly.

All this activity aside, the case does not stop in the period of time between the preliminary meeting and the hearing.

Following the preliminary meeting, if held, otherwise following his appointment, the arbitrator will issue an Order which will cover much of the process of the arbitration. The following is a typical but not necessarily complete Order which might be issued:

IN THE MATTER OF THE ARBITRATION ACT 1996
AND IN THE MATTER OF AN ARBITRATION BETWEEN

Claimant

and

Respondent

Upon hearing both parties
I DIRECT THAT
There will be pleadings in this arbitration as follows:
The Parties shall communicate with the Arbitrator, only in writing, and any such communication shall be served simultaneously upon all other parties to this Arbitration. All documents served by one party upon the other shall be served either personally or by means of the First Class Letter Post, in which case they shall also be delivered under the Recorded Delivery service. Service shall be effective if made at the address registered as that of the party, when appointing me as Arbitrator. A communication sent by Recorded Delivery First Class Letter Post shall be deemed served twenty four hours after it was posted unless such shall fall upon a weekend or public holiday in which case the letter will be deemed served the day following such weekend or public holiday.
Points of Claim will be delivered within 28 days from this date.
Points of Defence to be delivered within 28 days of delivery of the Points of Claim.
[*If there is a Counter Claim then the following may be inserted*]
Points of Reply to Counterclaim to be delivered within 28 days from the delivery of the Points of Counterclaim.
After the close of pleadings the Claimant and Respondent shall each deliver to the other within 14 days a list of documents which are or have been in

their possession or power which relate to the matters in this Arbitration, and inspection shall be given 14 days thereafter.
The conduct of the reference will be by way of a hearing at a venue to be agreed between the parties or if not agreed then at a venue to be decided upon by myself.
Experts will be limited to two on each side.
Exchange of Witness Statements will be by simultaneous mutual exchange within sixty days of the close of pleadings.
Within four weeks of the date of exchange of Witness Statements there shall be a simultaneous and mutual exchange of Expert Reports. Only witnesses whose statements are exchanged at this stage shall be able to give evidence at the hearing.
Within four weeks of the exchange of the Expert Reports, the experts shall be invited to a "without prejudice" meeting, following which they shall be invited to prepare a joint report containing details of the areas in which they agree and disagree.
Figures to be agreed as figures, plans, correspondence and photographs to be agreed as such in so far as is possible.
The parties shall prepare a bundle of documents suitably paginated and a copy of this bundle shall be delivered to me not later than seven days before the date of the hearing.
Liberty to either party to apply.

In all arbitrations as in all trials the sides will negotiate, and it is very rare for a case to reach a hearing; if it does, it is most improbable that the sides will not have resolved a very considerable amount of the issues in dispute, leaving only relatively minimal issues for the arbitrator to decide for them.

Assuming that the case does proceed to a hearing this will be on a specified day at a time and venue agreed by the parties or in default ordered by the arbitrator.

It is customary for the claimant to open the case, and whether he is acting in person or through an advocate, it is probable he will introduce himself and state who he appears for. It is helpful also for him to introduce any advocate for the other side. He will then provide a short opening speech indicating the issues in dispute.

Following this he will call his first witness.

Any witness called in an arbitration may be examined under oath and the arbitrator is empowered by law to administer any oath for the purposes of the examination of such a witness. The arbitrator is specifically not empowered to compel any witness to attend his hearing. The parties cannot be compelled to attend but if they fail to do so there are sanctions which can be used against them, which include striking out the case of the defaulting party.

As can be seen from this it is apparent that a witness cannot be

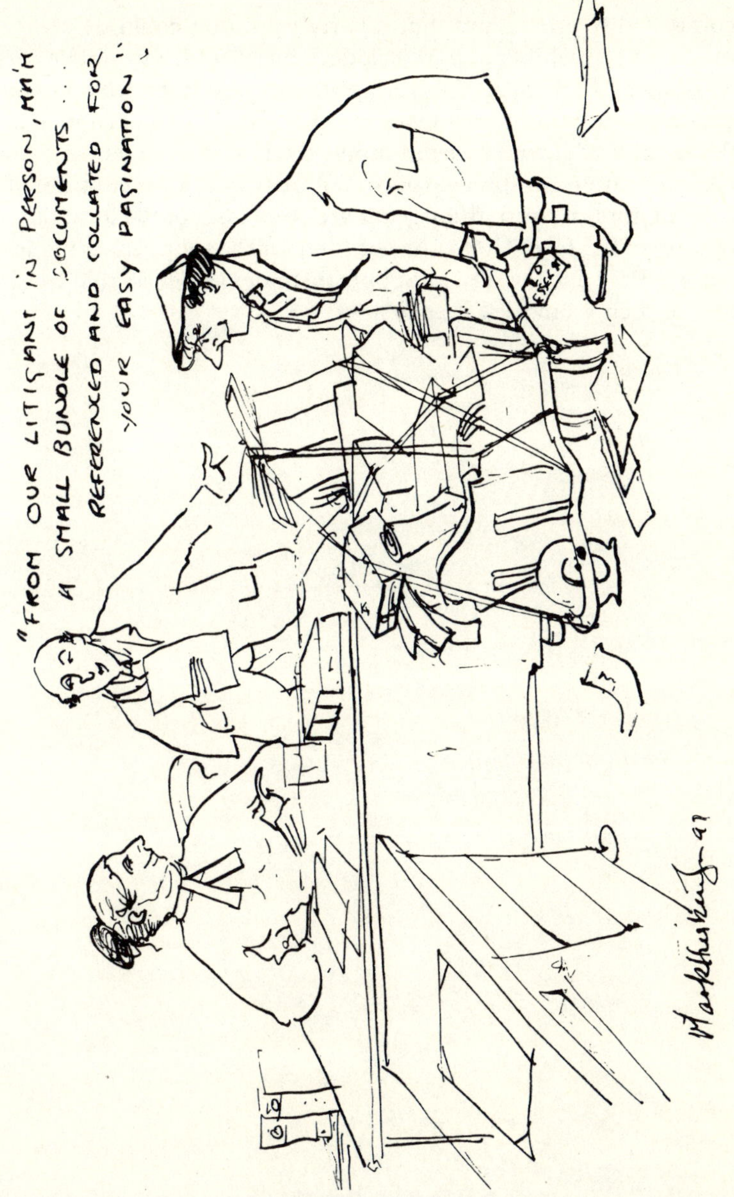

In providing the evidence it is of vital importance for the party to ensure that his or her evidence is concise and relevant and that documentation is easily referenced and available. It is no good providing a shoebox full of loose papers in the hope that the arbitrator and other party will miraculously be able to immediately find the relevant document.

compelled to attend and thus a party's position could be compromised by an inability to have evidence heard which would be to his assistance. Parliament has however ensured that this situation cannot occur by authorising the courts to issue writs of subpoena at the request of parties to arbitrations. Such writs compel the named person to attend as directed and a failure to comply is considered to be contempt of court. Subpoenas are issued out of the local district registry of the High Court. Application for the subpoena is made on a Form Praecipe for Writ of Subpoena under Order 38 rule 14. The text of such a Praecipe is as follows:

Praecipe for Writ of Subpoena (O. 38, r.14)

IN THE HIGH COURT OF JUSTICE **19 .— .—No.**

Division

[District Registry]

Between

Plaintiff

AND

Defendant

(1) Ad testificandum *or* duces tecum.
(2) Number of Witnesses.

Seal **Writ** of **Subpoena** (1)
for (2) Witnesses
on behalf of the

(3) Name of Witnesses.

directed to (3)

returnable

Dated this **day of** **19**

(Signed)
of

Agent for
of

Solicitor for the

HCE20/1

19 .— .—No.

IN THE HIGH COURT OF JUSTICE

Division

[

District Registry]

Praecipe Subpoena

Solicitor

Solicitor's Reference

OYEZ The Solicitors' Law Stationery Society Ltd., Oyez House, 7 Spa Road, London SE16 3QQ. 4.93 HCE20/2

High Court E20

The text of the actual subpoena depends upon whether or not the witness is to testify personally or is to bring documents or other items for the hearing. The **Subpoena Duces Tecum** is to be used for the production of items and the wording of it is as follows:

IN THE HIGH COURT OF JUSTICE 19 .– .– No:

Division

[District Registry]

Between

Claimant

and

Respondent

Elizabeth the Second, by the Grace of God, of the United Kingdom of Great Britain and Northern Ireland and of Our other realms and territories Queen, Head of the Commonwealth, Defender of the faith:
To: ***Name of Witness***
WE COMMAND YOU to attend at the sittings of the Arbitration at ***Insert address of premises where the Arbitration is to be held*** on the day fixed for the hearing of the above-named cause, notice of which will be given to you, and from day to day thereafter until the end of the hearing, to give evidence on behalf of the ***Insert here Claimant or Respondent***
AND WE ALSO COMMAND YOU to bring with you and produce at the place aforesaid on the day notified to you ***Insert here the description of documents or things to be produced***
Witness
Lord High Chancellor of Great Britain
the day of 19

It should be noted that the wording implies that the witness is commanded to give evidence and if such evidence is not required these words should be struck out.

If there is to be no production of documents but only oral evidence the correct Form of Subpoena is the **Subpoena ad testificandum**. The wording is slightly different and is reproduced below:

IN THE HIGH COURT OF JUSTICE 19 .– .– No:

Division

[District Registry]

Between

Claimant

and

Respondent

Elizabeth the Second, by the Grace of God, of the United Kingdom of Great Britain and Northern Ireland and of Our other realms and territories Queen, Head of the Commonwealth, Defender of the faith:
To: ***Name of Witness***
WE COMMAND YOU to attend at the sittings of the Arbitration at ***Insert address of premises where the Arbitration is to be held*** on the day fixed for the hearing of the above-named cause, notice of which will be given to you, and from day to day thereafter until the end of the hearing, to give evidence on behalf of the ***Insert here Claimant or Respondent***
Witness
Lord High Chancellor of Great Britain
the day of 19

A subpoena must be served personally upon the witness who must be provided with conduct money. The amount must be sufficient to allow him to travel to the court. If the subpoena is not served personally, unless certain other specific requirements have been complied with then it is not considered to have been validly served. A lack of conduct money or lack of sufficiency of conduct money also invalidates good service. Service must also have been made not less than four days before the witness is required to attend. It is important that these requirements are met if there is to be any sanction applied later by the court against the party for failure to comply with the terms of the subpoena.

The first witness, having been called, will be invited to take the Oath. If he objects he may Affirm; the words of the Oath and Affirmation are reproduced below. If a witness refuses to take any form of oath or affirmation the arbitrator may well attribute very little weight to the evidence provided by that witness.

The traditional wording of the Oath is:

> I swear by Almighty God that the evidence I shall give shall be the truth the whole truth and nothing but the truth.

The Oath administered by arbitrators is often worded as follows:

> I swear by Almighty God that the evidence which I shall give touching the matters in difference in this reference shall be the truth the whole truth and nothing but the truth.

The Oath is taken by the witness holding the New Testament in an uplifted hand (if he is a Christian), or holding the Old Testament (if Jewish). Other faiths may swear by their own deity, for example a Moslem will swear by Allah using the Koran, Hindus use the Bhagavad Gita, and members of other faiths will use their own holy book. Sometimes oaths are taken in ways which are inadvisable or difficult to implement. For example, there is a religion where the oath is taken by smashing a saucer; then the Nagas of Assam swear an oath by severing the head from a live animal with a single blow from a sword (a method to be used only if there is a slaughterhouse conveniently nearby and an absence of animal rights activists in the area).

In circumstances such as these, or if their holy book is not available, the witness may be invited to affirm. The affirmation is a strictly non-religious form of oath and the wording is as follows:

> I do solemnly sincerely and truly declare and affirm that the evidence I shall give shall be the truth the whole truth and nothing but the truth.

As mentioned earlier, if, having taken the oath, the witness provides evidence knowing it to be untrue, he is liable to be charged with perjury, an offence which carries a substantial custodial sentence.

Once the witness has been sworn, he will be asked to state his name, address and occupation. If he is an expert witness or professional witness his professional qualifications and current position will also be requested. A professional witness is a witness of fact, who holds special professional qualifications such as those of a doctor.

After these preliminaries, the witness will then be led through his witness statement by his advocate. This is termed examination in chief. After this the witness will then be cross-examined by the advocate for the other side. Cross-examination is the opportunity for the other side to explore the evidence in depth and to discredit both the witness and the evidence. There are rules about the way in which a witness can be personally discredited but even these allow the advocate a fair amount of leeway. The arbitrator will ensure that the witness is protected against flagrant abuse, and since no professional advocate will indulge in such discreditable behaviour the witness can look forward to being treated fairly.

After cross-examination follows re-examination, conducted by the advocate for the witness's side. This is the opportunity for the advocate to correct any misunderstandings that have arisen from the cross-examination. The arbitrator will be careful not to interfere with the advocate's style.

This procedure is repeated for each witness until all the witnesses for that side have given evidence.

Following this the other side is then able to provide the Tribunal with its evidence by calling its witnesses who will be treated in exactly the same manner.

After all the witnesses have been called the parties will make their closing speeches. On occasion the arbitrator will require that these speeches be reduced to written form.

Traditional wisdom is that the claimant's case is presented first, and that all witnesses of fact are excluded from the proceedings until they have given evidence whereas expert witnesses are generally permitted to be present throughout the whole of the proceedings. These "rules" are not however absolute, and variations are possible at the discretion of the arbitrator.

Other issues which arise in the arbitration relate to the matters of settlement and costs. Any party to an arbitration agreement is placed at risk of costs unless there is a further agreement between the parties as to how the costs shall be dealt with. Under the Arbitration Act it is not possible for parties to agree, in advance of a dispute arising, that if a dispute should arise one or other party will pay the costs of the arbitration regardless of the outcome. However, once a dispute has arisen, it is possible and proper for a party to agree with others to that dispute that they will indemnify all other parties in respect of all costs arising out of the arbitration. This having been said, it is an unusual form of agreement and in most cases the general rule relating to costs in an arbitration is that the loser pays all.

Where the costs are not fixed costs, as in a documents-only arbitration, the actual costs incurred can be quite considerable. They will involve not just the fees charged by the arbitrator, but the professional fees incurred by the losing side, and of course the similar costs incurred by the other side. These costs will include the legitimate costs of counsel and solicitors, the costs of the hire of the venue, the travelling expenses of parties and advocates, the cost of bringing witnesses to the tribunal, and the cost of instructing expert witnesses. Whilst this is not a full list of possible expenses, it provides an idea of the type and nature of the expenses which a losing party could face. The list is no less than the same party might face in litigation, with the exception of the arbitrator's fees. Judges are nearly but not quite free of charge. Recent Lord Chancellors have indulged in considerable thought about this and there is no doubt that the system is at considerable risk of review with inevitable savings to the exchequer.

Much cost will be incurred in the actual hearing and therefore any move which can reduce this must be welcomed.

In court proceedings there is a facility to make a "payment into court" which is a process whereby a defendant can pay an amount into the court which is less than is claimed by the plaintiff, but is a sum which the defendant thinks is justified as an offer of settlement. If the plaintiff achieves more than this sum at the final judgment, he will recover costs as usual. If, however, he is awarded a lesser sum than the payment in, he will not be able to recover costs for any of the action after the date of the payment into court made by the defendant.

There is no similar system established for the arbitration process and this is a definite weakness of the system, which many hoped would be remedied by the Arbitration Act 1996. It was not. Had it been the lawyers drafting the Bill could have done worse that enact legislation similar to that of the Hong Kong Arbitration Ordinance, which provides an identical system to that of court proceedings for dealing with this aspect of the process.

In England, the best that can happen is that there is a system known as the Calderbank Offer, which is a written offer made to the other side, incorporating the proposed terms of settlement. It is not shown to the arbitrator, who should have no knowledge of its existence, and no reference should be made to it during and after proceedings, assuming that it is not accepted. If the offer is accepted or if the offer is rejected and a lesser sum is awarded to the claimant, then when the arbitrator is apprised of the offer he will in determining costs act as if it had been a payment into court. The disadvantage of this system is that the offer is not backed by money, and whilst in most cases this does not matter it can be a cause for later dispute if the funds are not readily available.

The author has developed a system which approximates to a payment into court, with a reputable independent stakeholder taking the deposit of any funds in a similar manner to a payment into court, the effect being the same in terms of the monies and the ensuing arbitration.

The other protection for parties which is available in both arbitration proceedings and litigation is that they may have the costs of the proceedings taxed. This is not the use of the word tax in the sense that most people understand it but is a special legal sense in which the costs are assessed either by the arbitrator or by a court official known as a Taxing Master. Whoever undertakes this will consider each sum spent, decide whether it was reasonably incurred and, if having been reasonably incurred, whether it was a reasonable sum. If both these criteria are satisfied then the sum will be allowed and the party responsible for costs will have to pay it. If on the other hand the person taxing considers that the cost should not have been incurred, he may disallow it, in which case the party paying the sum cannot expect to recover it.

There are a number of criteria for taxing and for determining who pays what sums, but these will not be considered within the context of this book.

In most arbitrations, having heard the evidence the arbitrator will not give his decision and award immediately but will reserve his decision to a later stage. His award when it is published may take any form, but the following skeletal draft represents a typical format for a reasoned award.

A *[The arbitration agreement, date and parties]*
B *[The date and method of appointment of arbitrator]*
C *[The procedure adopted (Documents Only, or if Hearing give date)]*
D *[The issues]*
E *First issue of fact,* ***I find as a fact that . . . because the evidence of Mr X***

was more closely supported by the contemporaneous documents than that of Mr Y or I preferred the evidence of Mr Z to that of Mr A, or as appropriate.

F The first issue of law:

Argument for the Claimant . . .

Argument for the Respondent . . .

I prefer the case of the . . . because

(1) . . .

(2) . . .

I therefore find for the Claimant/ Respondent on this issue

G Second Issue (as first)

I therefore find for the Claimant/ Respondent on this issue

H **I therefore determine and award . . . with interest at . . . per cent from . . . to (the date of this award or as the case may be . . . per cent . . . from to . . .)**

J **(i) This Award is final as to all matters except costs.**

(ii) If either party wishes to make representations to me as to costs, it should send them to me, and to the other party, by noon on . . . If either party wishes to make any representations in answer to the other party's representations, it should send them to me and to the other party by noon on . . . Thereafter I will make my Final Award

K **I AWARD AND DETERMINE that the Claimant/Respondent shall pay to the Claimant/Respondent the costs of this Arbitration to be taxed (if not agreed) [by me] OR [in the High Court]**

One aspect of arbitration that is not fully appreciated by either the parties or their legal advisers is that an arbitrator can be empowered to provide not only a financial award but an Order for Specific Performance against a party. Specific performance means that the party subject to the Order is required and forced to perform a specific act. Such an act may be the dissolution of a partnership, or the removal of an obstruction to a right of way. This power is exceedingly helpful to parties as it means that the entire dispute can be be dealt with at the one time.

Finally if a party to the arbitration has reason to reject the award, he or she may apply to the court for an Order setting aside the award. The application must be made under Order 73 of the Rules of the Supreme Court, using form S38, which is reproduced below. This form is also utilised to make most applications in respect of an arbitration where the support or intervention of the court is requested. Details of the various reasons are not the subject of this book but may be sought from your legal adviser, who should in any event be consulted before an application of any sort is made to the court for support or intervention in arbitral proceedings.

Arbitration Application
In the High Court of Justice 19 No.
Queen's Bench Division
Commercial Court
(1) Use black ink and CAPITAL letters **Mercantile List** ([1]) **District Registry**

---

1. (i) In an arbitration application between

Applicant

and

Respondent

of

Respondent

of

Respondent

of

(ii) and in the matter of an (anticipated) arbitration between

Claimant

Respondent(s)

(2) Give name of any arbitrator(s) listed above as respondents or give full names and addresses where not named as respondents.

(iii) The arbitrator(s) to whom notice of this application is given are:([2])

---

(3) Delete (i) or (ii) as applicable.

Hearing ([3])

2. (i) This application is made on notice (ex parte).

(ii) The hearing of this application will take place in court (chambers)

on

at o'clock.

(or on a date to be fixed)

at ([4])

(4) Specify the court.

CHAPTER 7

ENFORCEMENT

This chapter relates to the enforcement of decisions made by tribunals and in particular arbitrators, and also deals with the enforcement of agreements reached by parties to a mediation.

In view of mediation being the less formal procedure, the author will deal with means of making such decisions enforceable and securing the finality which the parties desire.

As mentioned above, mediation is completely informal, in legal terms, and is a procedure whereby the parties to a dispute may negotiate until they reach an agreement between themselves as to how they wish to resolve the dispute. This will often produce a resolution which differs from that which would have been imposed at an adjudication in a court or by an arbitrator. The fact that mediation gives rise to the possibility of such eloquent resolutions, begs the question as to how they may be enforced.

The answer is indeed very simple! Parties to a dispute who reach an agreement on its resolution have come to a contractual agreement. Once finalised, this agreement is as binding upon them as any other contract. However, the fact that a dispute arose at all implies that at some point in time the parties failed to reach an amicable agreement and it would be tempting fate to expect them to suddenly change their attitudes and display an absolute, complete and total trust in each other.

It is therefore incumbent upon a mediator to ensure that prior to leaving a mediation where anything or everything has been agreed, by the parties, he should also ensure that they have, at least, committed to written form the agreement that they have concluded. It is only in this way that there is a complete understanding as to what has been agreed and there is no way of avoiding the agreement which is available to the party, short of breaching the written agreement.

It is this agreement that is so critical to the whole mediation process and it is also the time at which the lay party's legal representative can shine and assist both his party and any others to the mediation by drafting the agreement in simple, comprehensible and unambiguous terms. This is an art form which is to be most valued in any legal adviser, and which is not universally practised.

Assuming that the agreement is properly drafted then the parties are very unlikely to breach its terms but, if they do, then the other party has the option of enforcing an action in the courts for breach of contract.

There are, however, other ways to ensure the parties comply with the agreement. One method which has achieved considerable popularity with parties despite the fact that it is not without technical problems is the appointment of the mediator as an arbitrator to provide a consent award under the terms of the Arbitration Act 1996. The author has considerable experience of this and has found the technique exceedingly helpful where the parties, even after mediation, remain very distrustful of each other.

The effect of this is that the parties provide the mediator with a carefully drafted detail of the agreements they have reached. It is vital that if this is to be done every value figure and other important detail is correctly and clearly noted in writing and signed by BOTH or ALL parties to the mediation. Once this has been done, the parties then sign an appointment of the mediator as arbitrator. A suitable precedent appears in Chapter 6. The arbitrator will accept the appointment, again in written form, at which point the parties will be committed to the award which he makes.

The problem of non-compliance takes this chapter on to the enforcement of arbitral awards generally.

It is rare for parties to an arbitration not to comply with the terms of the award, but human nature being what it is the problem can and does happen.

As has been discussed earlier in this book, the courts try not to interfere with the process of arbitration and will only become involved in relatively few circumstances. These circumstances have been considerably reduced by the terms of the Arbitration Act 1996, which provide much more power for the arbitrator and less need for the parties to go to the courts for support of the process.

The only intervention of the courts which will be discussed in this chapter will be the power of the courts to enforce awards against parties who, for whatever reason, refuse to or are unable to comply with such an award.

It matters not if the award is a financial one or if the arbitrator has awarded specific performance, the court's ability to intervene is the same. However the enforcement of a financial debt is considerably easier than the enforcement of an Order for Specific Performance. There is no clear cut route specified in the legislation for the enforcement of specific performance as there is for the enforcement of a monetary award. This is not to say that such mechanisms do not exist, it is merely to warn the reader that in order to enforce such an award against a defaulter, the services of a solicitor will almost certainly be required.

The section of the Arbitration Act 1996 which provides for the enforcement of arbitral awards by the courts is section 66.

In discussing this aspect it is assumed that the arbitration has been undertaken in accordance with the terms of the Arbitration Act and that there is no challenge to the arbitrator or the award.

The first thing the party wishing to enforce the award should do is read it and ensure that the action he is demanding is the action which the award requires. Assuming that it is, then the party may register the award with the court having jurisdiction, most often the county court covering the area in which the award was made or the area in which the party lives or works.

The application to the court for enforcement of a monetary award is made using Form N322A.

Once the application is registered with the court and it has accepted jurisdiction, assuming it is satisfied as to the validity of the award and the absence of any appeal process it will then make an Order in the terms of the award obliging the defaulting party to comply.

It is in this way that enforcement can be made and the arbitral award is technically adopted as a judgment of the court. All means of enforcing a court judgment are available for enforcing the arbitral award in these circumstances.

Having read this, it may be helpful to the reader to have some idea of the possible powers that the court may exercise in enforcing a judgment. It is not intended that this be a comprehensive list and it will deal only superficially with the various powers the court has. Most of the comments will relate to the powers of the county court and it should be remembered that the High Court has greater and

Application for an Order to Recover Money Awarded by a Tribunal or Other Body

Application should be made to the Respondent's local court. If the Respondent resides out of England and Wales application must be made to the Applicant's local court.

1 Applicant's name and address

2 Name and address for service and payment (if different from above)

Ref/Tel No.

3 Respondent's name and address

4 Payment details

A	Amount of award	
B	Balance outstanding	
C	Interest since date of award (if any)* period [ ] rate [ ] %	
D	Court fee	
E	Solicitor's costs	
F	**Amount now due**	

*If the terms of the award entitle you to interest until the debt is paid, please state the daily rate of interest

£ [ ] per day

In the

County Court

For court use only

Case no:

Issue date:

Checklist

Answer the following questions, ticking the appropriate boxes

	Yes	No
• is a copy of the (tribunal) award attached?	☐	☐
• does the date of the award agree with the first date on the certificate?	☐	☐
• is the certificate signed and dated?	☐	☐
• is the amount at **4A** the same as the amount on the award?	☐	☐
• is the balance outstanding at 4B the same as or less than the amount of the award **4A**?	☐	☐
• do **4B**, **4C**, **4D** and **4E** add up to the amount given in box **4F**?	☐	☐

If you ticked the first box for every question, complete form N322 (Order for recovery of money awarded by tribunal).

The (proper) officer must sign this form before the order is sent out.

Signed

If you ticked the second box for any question, return the papers and fee to the sender (with an explanation if necessary).

5 Certificate

I wish to apply to recover in the county court the sum due under an award made against the Respondent dated , a copy of which is attached to this application.

I certify that the whole or part of the award has not been paid and that the balance now due is as shown.

Signed Applicant (Applicant's solicitor)

Dated

N322A Application for an Order to Recover Money Awarded by a Tribunal or Other Body (Order 25, rule 12)

9.93 CCN322A

County Court N322A

significantly wider powers available to itself as could well be anticipated.

Having made an Order it is anticipated that the respondent will comply. However this is often a far too simplistic approach and if the matter has got so far then it may well be expected that there will be further problems.

There are four major routes of enforcement which the court will utilise, which are:

A Warrant of Execution—This is an Order issued by the court enabling bailiffs to visit the defendant's home or business premises. Upon visiting, the bailiff will attempt to obtain payment by collecting the monies due from the party or he will seize goods for sale at auction. This method of enforcement has a limited success rate and those well versed in the system know of many ways in which this form of enforcement can be avoided entirely or the evil day put off. It is not a method which is universally commendable.

An Attachment of Earnings Order—This type of Order is an Order of the court to the employer of an adjudged defendant that he should deduct monies from the debtor's salary and make payments direct to the court. Needless to say the method is unpopular with employers who yet again have to act as agents for "state deductions" and in any event they tend not to appreciate employees who are the subject of court actions. Employees are also loath to identify employers and some will take the extreme action of becoming unemployed rather than pay the money. This method is therefore again fraught with difficulties for the claimant.

A Garnishee Order—This is an Order which attaches the judgment Order to the defendant's bank account to stop the defendant withdrawing sums from that account. It is also applicable to other accounts such as building society accounts and may be made against a person who owes money to the defendant. Once the Order is in place the monies are paid to the creditor.

Finally there is a Charging Order—This Order is one which registers the debt against the defendant's house or land. He is then unable to sell the property unless the debt is paid. The disadvantage of this method is that nothing will be forthcoming until the property is sold and this could in theory be a period of many years.

As can be seen, enforcement through the county court is not without its problems, but it is the best that can be achieved under the present system. It is also the reason why so few debtors resort to the county court when they could and the reason so many debtors seem to thrive within the system.

As stated earlier, the High Court has more sophisticated powers but rarely will these fall within the reach of the majority of parties attempting to enforce an award, as nearly all claims are valued below the level at which the High Court would normally be involved.

In practice it is of comfort to most people who are involved in an arbitration that the number of people who actually default on the award is in reality a very small number. If you are one of those few unfortunates who is the victim of such behaviour, you are in a very small minority but nonetheless a very worried one. The most profitable course of action is to discuss the matter with your opponent and if he has been represented then contact his representative. If all else fails, you may have to resort to formal legal action, but if so it is possibly worth instructing a legal adviser if you have not already done so, as the intricacies of the legal system are such that a deep knowledge of it will enhance the prospects of success.

CHAPTER 8

WHY AND HOW ADR?

This chapter is again fairly brief but it is an important one because it is in this chapter that there is a discussion of the benefits and advantages of the various systems available to you.

It has been mentioned much earlier in this book that there will be times when the choice of method available to the party may be very limited and in making this comment the author would respectfully refer the reader to comments concerning the presence of an arbitration clause, or the insistence of the other party on pursuing a case through the courts.

However, this having been said, there remains a very considerable amount of choice available to participants in disputes.

There now follows a short but concise approach to the distinctions between ADR and litigation which will be useful in helping the reader decide how such processes may be utilised.

Litigation is the word used for proceedings in the courts of law. The end result is binding upon the participants and enforceable against a defaulting party.

Arbitration is the system whereby parties agree to appoint a "private judge" to provide a binding award which is of itself enforceable as an adjudication of the courts.

Mediation is a method of negotiation which does not affect the outcome of the dispute unless and until the parties wish it.

Thus it follows that it is not possible to have the same issue decided by both arbitration and litigation, although the parties may invoke mediation at any stage in either of these processes.

The decision to follow the dispute through litigation is usually the decision of the injured party and in most cases once this is commenced the parties will be committed to following this particular course of action. This does not, of course, mean that it must be followed through to the bitter end, namely a trial, since the introduction of mediation might well resolve the issues at some point in the procedure.

If the party who is being sued can show that the matter should have been dealt with through arbitration rather than litigation, it is open to that party to make an application to the court to stay the litigation proceedings in order that the matter may be dealt with by arbitration. Remember that if you are bound by prior agreement to submit the matter to arbitration you will not be able to obtain legal aid to cover the costs, even if you would be eligible for it in respect of litigation proceedings. You may have legal expense insurance which will cover the cost. This may be an opportune moment to see if you are in fact covered by such insurance and, if not, seek professional advice from your insurance broker as to the way in which you can protect your interests against such risks.

Whether or not you have such protection, if you are involved in a dispute and regardless of whether proceedings of any sort (arbitration or litigation) have been commenced, then it is worth considering the possibility of submitting the whole issue to mediation.

In choosing a method of resolving your dispute there are a considerable number of factors to take into account. In any dispute probably the most important factor to consider is the strength of your case. It is no use pursuing a case if eventually you are going to lose. The effect of losing a legal battle can be both emotionally and financially crippling, and principles, whilst excellent to hold, are exceedingly expensive to defend. The cost of setting out to fight an opponent as a matter of principle is one way of ensuring that there is a prolonged and expensive battle with no certain end where the only certain fact is that both parties will suffer financially to an extent which neither could possibly have anticipated. In law there is no certain outcome and a trivial fact overlooked by all until accidentally presented by a party can swing the outcome in a way which ten minutes before was not even in the contemplation of any of the parties.

It can be seen from this that settling a dispute is the next best thing to avoiding it. If you are unlucky enough to fall into a potential dispute, move very carefully and seek, if appropriate, the best advice from the best professional advisers you can afford. In this way you may be prevented from embarking on what could be a devastating course of events.

If you take the next step and decide that you wish to pursue the case, or if your opponent commits you to defending a case, then review your position at each and every stage with the utmost care. If you are the defendant, as soon as you can you should decide whether to defend the case. If you decide you cannot win then make an early move to settle.

If you decide that your case is worth pursuing then whether plaintiff, defendant, claimant or respondent, look to see how costs can be mitigated and contemplate whether you could resolve the dispute by informal negotiation. If not, then consider the use of mediation.

Professional advisers may or may not encourage you to utilise alternative means of resolving disputes. Usually reticence is the result of a lack of knowledge of the procedure rather than a sound bit of professional advice. It is interesting to find how few professional advisers actually understand mediation or arbitration and if large numbers are questioned then only a few will be able to give a full explanation of the various systems. It therefore helps if the client has a full understanding and can give a cogent reason for wanting to explore the possibility of utilising ADR for the resolution of a particular dispute. There is no reason to doubt that within a very short time this situation will change and professional advisers will within the next two or three years both have a fuller understanding of and be making significant use of both arbitration and mediation.

If you believe that ADR in any of its forms might be of assistance then you should encourage your professional advisers to give extra consideration to your request and if they are of the opinion that it is not of use they should be asked to justify that advice fully.

Never forget the comments made earlier in the book concerning the use of a third party to approach the other side. This gives by far the greatest chance of the option being exercised.

Be careful to remember that if you refuse an offer from the other side to consider the use of mediation, then there is a strong probability that when it comes to taxation or agreement of costs this refusal will be used as a justification for reducing the costs you may claim. This may apply whether you win, lose or settle the case.

Always keep in your mind that the judge or arbitrator will make a decision which is binding upon you and that this decision will be made upon the evidence which is ACTUALLY presented to him for adjudication. It is no use remembering after the hearing that you should have given a piece of evidence. Once you have finished, your chance to introduce evidence is terminated and, no matter how persuasive, it will never be given.

It follows from this that you should treat any legal proceedings, whether through the courts or through arbitration, as being of the utmost importance and not a procedure to be trivialised. Make every effort to settle as there is no such thing as a predictable outcome.

There is much very helpful literature available through the courts for parties to litigation, and the available literature in conjunction with Citizens' Advice Bureaux, law centres and from companies specialising in dispute resolution will do much to educate parties. Additionally many companies will give advice to persons contemplating the use of alternative means of resolving a dispute.

APPENDICES

APPENDIX 1

SAMPLE LETTERS

Letter to debtor whose account is overdue

Dear

Re: (*Insert here the date and number of your invoice and the value of it*)

I (We if writing on behalf of a company) note from our records that the above mentioned invoice remains unpaid. It would be much appreciated if you could send your remittance to me/us without further delay.

It is of course possible that our records are incorrect and that you have already paid or that your payment has crossed in the post with this letter. If this is the case please let me/us know immediately in order that I/we may amend our records.

Yours faithfully

Second Letter to Debtor who has failed to respond to first letter within a reasonable time (seven days). This letter should be sent by Recorded Delivery post

Dear

Re: (*Insert here the date and number of your invoice and the value of it*)

I/We wrote to you on (*insert here the date of your last letter*). No response has been received and in case you did not receive it I/we am/are enclosing a copy for your information.

In any event I/we must insist that you make payment of the outstanding sum within seven days or I/we will be forced to take steps to recover the debt through the courts.

I/We trust that this form of action will not prove necessary and in view of the damage such action could do to your reputation it is hoped that your payment will be received without further delay.

It is respectfully suggested that any payment to us should be sent by means of the Recorded Delivery post and if you are sending cash then Registered Post should be used.

Yours faithfully,

Letter Before Action

Dear

I write to advise you that it is my intention to commence legal proceedings against you as a result of your (*insert here the simple details of the claim e.g. negligence, in that on the 3rd day of May 1998, you caused me injury and damaged my car by reason of your negligent driving. I sustained both damage to my car and personal injuries which are quantified as follows; Damage to car £2345.98, cost of hire car, required during period of time car was being repaired £124.56, Personal Injuries, I sustained a whip lash injury to my neck £3200.00, loss of wages caused by absence from work for three weeks £523.00*).

An alternative version might be (*As a result of your failure to comply with the terms of the contract you entered into with myself, I have sustained losses amounting to £9780.06, the loss arising from your failure to deliver the product as detailed in the contract.*)

Unless I receive the aforesaid sums within a period of 14 days from the date of this letter I shall have no alternative but to issue proceedings against you.

Should you wish to nominate solicitors to accept proceedings on your behalf please write and advise of their details within the period of fourteen days.

Yours faithfully,

APPENDIX 2

ARBITRATION ACT 1996

ARRANGEMENT OF SECTIONS

PART I ARBITRATION PURSUANT TO AN ARBITRATION AGREEMENT

The arbitral tribunal

Jurisdiction of the arbitral tribunal

The arbitral proceedings

Powers of court in relation to arbitral proceedings

The award

Costs of the arbitration

Powers of the court in relation to award

Miscellaneous

Supplementary

PART II OTHER PROVISIONS RELATING TO ARBITRATION

Domestic arbitration agreements

Consumer arbitration agreements

Schedules

PART I ARBITRATION PURSUANT TO AN ARBITRATION AGREEMENT

INTRODUCTORY

General principles

1. The provisions of this Part are founded on the following principles, and shall be construed accordingly—

(a) the object of arbitration is to obtain the fair resolution of disputes by an impartial tribunal without unnecessary delay or expense;

(b) the parties should be free to agree how their disputes are resolved, subject only to such safeguards as are necessary in the public interest;

(c) in matters governed by this Part the court should not intervene except as provided by this Part.

Scope of application of provisions

2.—(1) The provisions of this Part apply where the seat of the arbitration is in England and Wales or Northern Ireland.

(2) The following sections apply even if the seat of the arbitration is outside England and Wales or Northern Ireland or no seat has been designated or determined—

(a) sections 9 to 11 (stay of legal proceedings, &c.), and

(b) section 66 (enforcement of arbitral awards).

(3) The powers conferred by the following sections apply even if

the seat of the arbitration is outside England and Wales or Northern Ireland or no seat has been designated or determined—

(a) section 43 (securing the attendance of witnesses), and

(b) section 44 (court powers exercisable in support of arbitral proceedings);

but the court may refuse to exercise any such power if, in the opinion of the court, the fact that the seat of the arbitration is outside England and Wales or Northern Ireland, or that when designated or determined the seat is likely to be outside England and Wales or Northern Ireland, makes it inappropriate to do so.

(4) The court may exercise a power conferred by any provision of this Part not mentioned in subsection (2) or (3) for the purpose of supporting the arbitral process where—

(a) no seat of the arbitration has been designated or determined, and

(b) by reason of a connection with England and Wales or Northern Ireland the court is satisfied that it is appropriate to do so.

(5) Section 7 (separability of arbitration agreement) and section 8 (death of a party) apply where the law applicable to the arbitration agreement is the law of England and Wales or Northern Ireland even if the seat of the arbitration is outside England and Wales or Northern Ireland or has not been designated or determined.

The seat of the arbitration

3. In this Part "the seat of the arbitration" means the juridical seat of the arbitration designated—

(a) by the parties to the arbitration agreement, or

(b) by any arbitral or other institution or person vested by the parties with powers in that regard, or

(c) by the arbitral tribunal if so authorised by the parties,

or determined, in the absence of any such designation, having regard to the parties' agreement and all the relevant circumstances.

Mandatory and non-mandatory provisions

4.—(1) The mandatory provisions of this Part are listed in Schedule 1 and have effect notwithstanding any agreement to the contrary.

(2) The other provisions of this Part (the "non-mandatory

provisions") allow the parties to make their own arrangements by agreement but provide rules which apply in the absence of such agreement.

(3) The parties may make such arrangements by agreeing to the application of institutional rules or providing any other means by which a matter may be decided.

(4) It is immaterial whether or not the law applicable to the parties' agreement is the law of England and Wales or, as the case may be, Northern Ireland.

(5) The choice of a law other than the law of England and Wales or Northern Ireland as the applicable law in respect of a matter provided for by a non-mandatory provision of this Part is equivalent to an agreement making provision about that matter.

For this purpose an applicable law determined in accordance with the parties' agreement, or which is objectively determined in the absence of any express or implied choice, shall be treated as chosen by the parties.

Agreements to be in writing

5.—(1) The provisions of this Part apply only where the arbitration agreement is in writing, and any other agreement between the parties as to any matter is effective for the purposes of this Part only if in writing.

The expressions "agreement", "agree" and "agreed" shall be construed accordingly.

(2) There is an agreement in writing—

- (a) if the agreement is made in writing (whether or not it is signed by the parties),
- (b) if the agreement is made by exchange of communications in writing, or
- (c) if the agreement is evidenced in writing.

(3) Where parties agree otherwise than in writing by reference to terms which are in writing, they make an agreement in writing.

(4) An agreement is evidenced in writing if an agreement made otherwise than in writing is recorded by one of the parties, or by a third party, with the authority of the parties to the agreement.

(5) An exchange of written submissions in arbitral or legal proceedings in which the existence of an agreement otherwise than in writing is alleged by one party against another party and not

denied by the other party in his response constitutes as between those parties an agreement in writing to the effect alleged.

(6) References in this Part to anything being written or in writing include its being recorded by any means.

THE ARBITRATION AGREEMENT

Definition of arbitration agreement

6.—(1) In this Part an "arbitration agreement" means an agreement to submit to arbitration present or future disputes (whether they are contractual or not).

(2) The reference in an agreement to a written form of arbitration clause or to a document containing an arbitration clause constitutes an arbitration agreement if the reference is such as to make that clause part of the agreement.

Separability of arbitration agreement

7. Unless otherwise agreed by the parties, an arbitration agreement which forms or was intended to form part of another agreement (whether or not in writing) shall not be regarded as invalid, non-existent or ineffective because that other agreement is invalid, or did not come into existence or has become ineffective, and it shall for that purpose be treated as a distinct agreement.

Whether agreement discharged by death of party

8.—(1) Unless otherwise agreed by the parties, an arbitration agreement is not discharged by the death of a party and may be enforced by or against the personal representatives of that party.

(2) Subsection (1) does not affect the operation of any enactment or rule of law by virtue of which a substantive right or obligation is extinguished by death.

STAY OF LEGAL PROCEEDINGS

Stay of legal proceedings

9.—(1) A party to an arbitration agreement against whom legal proceedings are brought (whether by way of claim or counterclaim) in respect of a matter which under the agreement is to be referred to arbitration may (upon notice to the other parties to the proceedings) apply to the court in which the proceedings have been brought to stay the proceedings so far as they concern that matter.

(2) An application may be made notwithstanding that the matter is to be referred to arbitration only after the exhaustion of other dispute resolution procedures.

(3) An application may not be made by a person before taking the appropriate procedural step (if any) to acknowledge the legal proceedings against him or after he has taken any step in those proceedings to answer the substantive claim.

(4) On an application under this section the court shall grant a stay unless satisfied that the arbitration agreement is null and void, inoperative, or incapable of being performed.

(5) If the court refuses to stay the legal proceedings, any provision that an award is a condition precedent to the bringing of legal proceedings in respect of any matter is of no effect in relation to those proceedings.

Reference of interpleader issue to arbitration

10.—(1) Where in legal proceedings relief by way of interpleader is granted and any issue between the claimants is one in respect of which there is an arbitration agreement between them, the court granting the relief shall direct that the issue be determined in accordance with the agreement unless the circumstances are such that proceedings brought by a claimant in respect of the matter would not be stayed.

(2) Where subsection (1) applies but the court does not direct that the issue be determined in accordance with the arbitration agreement, any provision that an award is a condition precedent to the bringing of legal proceedings in respect of any matter shall not affect the determination of that issue by the court.

Retention of security where Admiralty proceedings stayed

11.—(1) Where Admiralty proceedings are stayed on the ground that the dispute in question should be submitted to arbitration, the court granting the stay may, if in those proceedings property has been arrested or bail or other security has been given to prevent or obtain release from arrest—

(a) order that the property arrested be retained as security for the satisfaction of any award given in the arbitration in respect of that dispute, or
(b) order that the stay of those proceedings be conditional on the provision of equivalent security for the satisfaction of any such award.

(2) Subject to any provision made by rules of court and to any necessary modifications, the same law and practice shall apply in relation to property retained in pursuance of an order as would apply if it were held for the purposes of proceedings in the court making the order.

COMMENCEMENT OF ARBITRAL PROCEEDINGS

Power of court to extend time for beginning arbitral proceedings, &c.

12.—(1) Where an arbitration agreement to refer future disputes to arbitration provides that a claim shall be barred, or the claimant's right extinguished, unless the claimant takes within a time fixed by the agreement some step—

(a) to begin arbitral proceedings, or
(b) to begin other dispute resolution procedures which must be exhausted before arbitral proceedings can be begun,

the court may by order extend the time for taking that step.

(2) Any party to the arbitration agreement may apply for such an order (upon notice to the other parties), but only after a claim has arisen and after exhausting any available arbitral process for obtaining an extension of time.

(3) The court shall make an order only if satisfied—

(a) that the circumstances are such as were outside the reasonable contemplation of the parties when they agreed the provision in question, and that it would be just to extend the time, or
(b) that the conduct of one party makes it unjust to hold the other party to the strict terms of the provision in question.

(4) The court may extend the time for such period and on such terms as it thinks fit, and may do so whether or not the time previously fixed (by agreement or by a previous order) has expired.

(5) An order under this section does not affect the operation of the Limitation Acts (see section 13).

(6) The leave of the court is required for any appeal from a decision of the court under this section.

Application of Limitation Acts

13.—(1) The Limitation Acts apply to arbitral proceedings as they apply to legal proceedings.

(2) The court may order that in computing the time prescribed by the Limitation Acts for the commencement of proceedings (including arbitral proceedings) in respect of a dispute which was the subject matter—

(a) of an award which the court orders to be set aside or declares to be of no effect, or

(b) of the affected part of an award which the court orders to be set aside in part, or declares to be in part of no effect,

the period between the commencement of the arbitration and the date of the order referred to in paragraph (a) or (b) shall be excluded.

(3) In determining for the purposes of the Limitation Acts when a cause of action accrued, any provision that an award is a condition precedent to the bringing of legal proceedings in respect of a matter to which an arbitration agreement applies shall be disregarded.

(4) In this Part "the Limitation Acts" means—

(a) in England and Wales, the Limitation Act 1980, the Foreign Limitation Periods Act 1984 and any other enactment (whenever passed) relating to the limitation of actions;

(b) in Northern Ireland, the Limitation (Northern Ireland) Order 1989, the Foreign Limitation Periods (Northern Ireland) Order 1985 and any other enactment (whenever passed) relating to the limitation of actions.

Commencement of arbitral proceedings

14.—(1) The parties are free to agree when arbitral proceedings are to be regarded as commenced for the purposes of this Part and for the purposes of the Limitation Acts.

(2) If there is no such agreement the following provisions apply.

(3) Where the arbitrator is named or designated in the arbitration agreement, arbitral proceedings are commenced in respect of a matter when one party serves on the other party or parties a notice in writing requiring him or them to submit that matter to the person so named or designated.

(4) Where the arbitrator or arbitrators are to be appointed by the parties, arbitral proceedings are commenced in respect of a matter when one party serves on the other party or parties notice in writing

requiring him or them to appoint an arbitrator or to agree to the appointment of an arbitrator in respect of that matter.

(5) Where the arbitrator or arbitrators are to be appointed by a person other than a party to the proceedings, arbitral proceedings are commenced in respect of a matter when one party gives notice in writing to that person requesting him to make the appointment in respect of that matter.

THE ARBITRAL TRIBUNAL

The arbitral tribunal

15.—(1) The parties are free to agree on the number of arbitrators to form the tribunal and whether there is to be a chairman or umpire.

(2) Unless otherwise agreed by the parties, an agreement that the number of arbitrators shall be two or any other even number shall be understood as requiring the appointment of an additional arbitrator as chairman of the tribunal.

(3) If there is no agreement as to the number of arbitrators, the tribunal shall consist of a sole arbitrator.

Procedure for appointment of arbitrators

16.—(1) The parties are free to agree on the procedure for appointing the arbitrator or arbitrators, including the procedure for appointing any chairman or umpire.

(2) If or to the extent that there is no such agreement, the following provisions apply.

(3) If the tribunal is to consist of a sole arbitrator, the parties shall jointly appoint the arbitrator not later than 28 days after service of a request in writing by either party to do so.

(4) If the tribunal is to consist of two arbitrators, each party shall appoint one arbitrator not later than 14 days after service of a request in writing by either party to do so.

(5) If the tribunal is to consist of three arbitrators—

(a) each party shall appoint one arbitrator not later than 14 days after service of a request in writing by either party to do so, and

(b) the two so appointed shall forthwith appoint a third arbitrator as the chairman of the tribunal.

(6) If the tribunal is to consist of two arbitrators and an umpire—

(a) each party shall appoint one arbitrator not later than 14 days after service of a request in writing by either party to do so, and

(b) the two so appointed may appoint an umpire at any time after they themselves are appointed and shall do so before any substantive hearing or forthwith if they cannot agree on a matter relating to the arbitration.

(7) In any other case (in particular, if there are more than two parties) section 18 applies as in the case of a failure of the agreed appointment procedure.

Power in case of default to appoint sole arbitrator

17.—(1) Unless the parties otherwise agree, where each of two parties to an arbitration agreement is to appoint an arbitrator and one party ("the party in default") refuses to do so, or fails to do so within the time specified, the other party, having duly appointed his arbitrator, may give notice in writing to the party in default that he proposes to appoint his arbitrator to act as sole arbitrator.

(2) If the party in default does not within 7 clear days of that notice being given—

(a) make the required appointment, and

(b) notify the other party that he has done so,

the other party may appoint his arbitrator as sole arbitrator whose award shall be binding on both parties as if he had been so appointed by agreement.

(3) Where a sole arbitrator has been appointed under subsection (2), the party in default may (upon notice to the appointing party) apply to the court which may set aside the appointment.

(4) The leave of the court is required for any appeal from a decision of the court under this section.

Failure of appointment procedure

18.—(1) The parties are free to agree what is to happen in the event of a failure of the procedure for the appointment of the arbitral tribunal.

There is no failure if an appointment is duly made under section 17 (power in case of default to appoint sole arbitrator), unless that appointment is set aside.

(2) If or to the extent that there is no such agreement any party to the arbitration agreement may (upon notice to the other parties) apply to the court to exercise its powers under this section.

(3) Those powers are—

(a) to give directions as to the making of any necessary appointments;

(b) to direct that the tribunal shall be constituted by such appointments (or any one or more of them) as have been made;

(c) to revoke any appointments already made;

(d) to make any necessary appointments itself.

(4) An appointment made by the court under this section has effect as if made with the agreement of the parties.

(5) The leave of the court is required for any appeal from a decision of the court under this section.

Court to have regard to agreed qualifications

19. In deciding whether to exercise, and in considering how to exercise, any of its powers under section 16 (procedure for appointment of arbitrators) or section 18 (failure of appointment procedure), the court shall have due regard to any agreement of the parties as to the qualifications required of the arbitrators.

Chairman

20.—(1) Where the parties have agreed that there is to be a chairman, they are free to agree what the functions of the chairman are to be in relation to the making of decisions, orders and awards.

(2) If or to the extent that there is no such agreement, the following provisions apply.

(3) Decisions, orders and awards shall be made by all or a majority of the arbitrators (including the chairman).

(4) The view of the chairman shall prevail in relation to a decision, order or award in respect of which there is neither unanimity nor a majority under subsection (3).

Umpire

21.—(1) Where the parties have agreed that there is to be an umpire, they are free to agree what the functions of the umpire are to be, and in particular—

(a) whether he is to attend the proceedings, and
(b) when he is to replace the other arbitrators as the tribunal with power to make decisions, orders and awards.

(2) If or to the extent that there is no such agreement, the following provisions apply.

(3) The umpire shall attend the proceedings and be supplied with the same documents and other materials as are supplied to the other arbitrators.

(4) Decisions, orders and awards shall be made by the other arbitrators unless and until they cannot agree on a matter relating to the arbitration.

In that event they shall forthwith give notice in writing to the parties and the umpire, whereupon the umpire shall replace them as the tribunal with power to make decisions, orders and awards as if he were sole arbitrator.

(5) If the arbitrators cannot agree but fail to give notice of that fact, or if any of them fails to join in the giving of notice, any party to the arbitral proceedings may (upon notice to the other parties and to the tribunal) apply to the court which may order that the umpire shall replace the other arbitrators as the tribunal with power to make decisions, orders and awards as if he were sole arbitrator.

(6) The leave of the court is required for any appeal from a decision of the court under this section.

Decision-making where no chairman or umpire

22.—(1) Where the parties agree that there shall be two or more arbitrators with no chairman or umpire, the parties are free to agree how the tribunal is to make decisions, orders and awards.

(2) If there is no such agreement, decisions, orders and awards shall be made by all or a majority of the arbitrators.

Revocation of arbitrator's authority

23.—(1) The parties are free to agree in what circumstances the authority of an arbitrator may be revoked.

(2) If or to the extent that there is no such agreement the following provisions apply.

(3) The authority of an arbitrator may not be revoked except—

(a) by the parties acting jointly, or

(b) by an arbitral or other institution or person vested by the parties with powers in that regard.

(4) Revocation of the authority of an arbitrator by the parties acting jointly must be agreed in writing unless the parties also agree (whether or not in writing) to terminate the arbitration agreement.

(5) Nothing in this section affects the power of the court—

(a) to revoke an appointment under section 18 (powers exercisable in case of failure of appointment procedure), or

(b) to remove an arbitrator on the grounds specified in section 24.

Power of court to remove arbitrator

24.—(1) A party to arbitral proceedings may (upon notice to the other parties, to the arbitrator concerned and to any other arbitrator) apply to the court to remove an arbitrator on any of the following grounds—

(a) that circumstances exist that give rise to justifiable doubts as to his impartiality;

(b) that he does not possess the qualifications required by the arbitration agreement;

(c) that he is physically or mentally incapable of conducting the proceedings or there are justifiable doubts as to his capacity to do so;

(d) that he has refused or failed—

(i) properly to conduct the proceedings, or

(ii) to use all reasonable despatch in conducting the proceedings or making an award,

and that substantial injustice has been or will be caused to the applicant.

(2) If there is an arbitral or other institution or person vested by the parties with power to remove an arbitrator, the court shall not exercise its power of removal unless satisfied that the applicant has first exhausted any available recourse to that institution or person.

(3) The arbitral tribunal may continue the arbitral proceedings and make an award while an application to the court under this section is pending.

(4) Where the court removes an arbitrator, it may make such order as it thinks fit with respect to his entitlement (if any) to fees or expenses, or the repayment of any fees or expenses already paid.

(5) The arbitrator concerned is entitled to appear and be heard by the court before it makes any order under this section.

(6) The leave of the court is required for any appeal from a decision of the court under this section.

Resignation of arbitrator

25.—(1) The parties are free to agree with an arbitrator as to the consequences of his resignation as regards—

(a) his entitlement (if any) to fees or expenses, and
(b) any liability thereby incurred by him.

(2) If or to the extent that there is no such agreement the following provisions apply.

(3) An arbitrator who resigns his appointment may (upon notice to the parties) apply to the court—

(a) to grant him relief from any liability thereby incurred by him, and
(b) to make such order as it thinks fit with respect to his entitlement (if any) to fees or expenses or the repayment of any fees or expenses already paid.

(4) If the court is satisfied that in all the circumstances it was reasonable for the arbitrator to resign, it may grant such relief as is mentioned in subsection (3)(a) on such terms as it thinks fit.

(5) The leave of the court is required for any appeal from a decision of the court under this section.

Death of arbitrator or person appointing him

26.—(1) The authority of an arbitrator is personal and ceases on his death.

(2) Unless otherwise agreed by the parties, the death of the person by whom an arbitrator was appointed does not revoke the arbitrator's authority.

Filling of vacancy, &c.

27.—(1) Where an arbitrator ceases to hold office, the parties are free to agree—

(a) whether and if so how the vacancy is to be filled,
(b) whether and if so to what extent the previous proceedings should stand, and

(c) what effect (if any) his ceasing to hold office has on any appointment made by him (alone or jointly).

(2) If or to the extent that there is no such agreement, the following provisions apply.

(3) The provisions of sections 16 (procedure for appointment of arbitrators) and 18 (failure of appointment procedure) apply in relation to the filling of the vacancy as in relation to an original appointment.

(4) The tribunal (when reconstituted) shall determine whether and if so to what extent the previous proceedings should stand.

This does not affect any right of a party to challenge those proceedings on any ground which had arisen before the arbitrator ceased to hold office.

(5) His ceasing to hold office does not affect any appointment by him (alone or jointly) of another arbitrator, in particular any appointment of a chairman or umpire.

Joint and several liability of parties to arbitrators for fees and expenses

28.—(1) The parties are jointly and severally liable to pay to the arbitrators such reasonable fees and expenses (if any) as are appropriate in the circumstances.

(2) Any party may apply to the court (upon notice to the other parties and to the arbitrators) which may order that the amount of the arbitrators' fees and expenses shall be considered and adjusted by such means and upon such terms as it may direct.

(3) If the application is made after any amount has been paid to the arbitrators by way of fees or expenses, the court may order the repayment of such amount (if any) as is shown to be excessive, but shall not do so unless it is shown that it is reasonable in the circumstances to order repayment.

(4) The above provisions have effect subject to any order of the court under section 24(4) or 25(3)(b) (order as to entitlement to fees or expenses in case of removal or resignation of arbitrator).

(5) Nothing in this section affects any liability of a party to any other party to pay all or any of the costs of the arbitration (see sections 59 to 65) or any contractual right of an arbitrator to payment of his fees and expenses.

(6) In this section references to arbitrators include an arbitrator

who has ceased to act and an umpire who has not replaced the other arbitrators.

Immunity of arbitrator

29.—(1) An arbitrator is not liable for anything done or omitted in the discharge or purported discharge of his functions as arbitrator unless the act or omission is shown to have been in bad faith.

(2) Subsection (1) applies to an employee or agent of an arbitrator as it applies to the arbitrator himself.

(3) This section does not affect any liability incurred by an arbitrator by reason of his resigning (but see section 25).

JURISDICTION OF THE ARBITRAL TRIBUNAL

Competence of tribunal to rule on its own jurisdiction

30.—(1) Unless otherwise agreed by the parties, the arbitral tribunal may rule on its own substantive jurisdiction, that is, as to—

(a) whether there is a substantive arbitration agreement,
(b) whether the tribunal is properly constituted, and
(c) what matters have been submitted to arbitration in accordance with the arbitration agreement.

(2) Any such ruling may be challenged by any available arbitral process of appeal or review or in accordance with the provisions of this Part.

Objection to substantive jurisdiction of the tribunal

31.—(1) An objection that the arbitral tribunal lacks substantive jurisdiction at the outset of the proceedings must be raised by a party not later than the time he takes the first step in the proceedings to contest the merits of any matter in relation to which he challenges the tribunal's jurisdiction.

A party is not precluded from raising such an objection by the fact that he has appointed or participated in the appointment of the arbitrator.

(2) Any objection during the course of the arbitral proceedings that the arbitral tribunal is exceeding its substantive jurisdiction must be made as soon as possible after the matter alleged to be beyond its jurisdiction is raised.

(3) The arbitral tribunal may admit an objection later than the

time specified in subsection (1) or (2) if it considers the delay justified.

(4) Where an objection is duly taken to the tribunal's substantive jurisdiction and the tribunal has power to rule on its own jurisdiction, it may—

(a) rule on the matter in an award as to jurisdiction;

(b) deal with the objection in its award on the merits.

If the parties agree which of these courses the tribunal should take, the tribunal shall proceed accordingly.

(5) The tribunal may in any case, and shall if the parties so agree, stay proceedings whilst an application is made to the court under section 32 (determination of preliminary point of jurisdiction).

Determination of preliminary point of jurisdiction

32.—(1) The court may, on the application of a party to arbitral proceedings (upon notice to the other parties), determine any questions as to the substantive jurisdiction of the tribunal.

A party may lose the right to object (see section 73).

(2) An application under this section shall not be considered unless—

(a) it is made with the agreement in writing of all the other parties to the proceedings, or

(b) it is made with the permission of the tribunal and the court is satisfied—

(i) that the determination of the question is likely to produce substantial savings in costs,

(ii) that the application was made without delay,

(iii) that there is good reason why the matter should be decided by the court.

(3) An application under this section, unless made with the agreement of all the other parties to the proceedings, shall state the grounds on which it is said that the matter should be decided by the court.

(4) Unless otherwise agreed by the parties, the arbitral tribunal may continue the arbitral proceedings and make an award while an application to the court under this section is pending.

(5) Unless the court gives leave, no appeal lies from a decision of the court whether the conditions specified in subsection (2) are met.

(6) The decision of the court on the question of jurisdiction shall be treated as a judgment of the court for the purposes of an appeal.

But no appeal lies without the leave of the court which shall not be given unless the court considers that the question involves a point of law which is one of general importance or is one which for some other special reason should be considered by the Court of Appeal.

THE ARBITRAL PROCEEDINGS

General duty of the tribunal

33.—(1) The tribunal shall—

(a) act fairly and impartially as between the parties, giving each party a reasonable opportunity of putting his case and dealing with that of his opponent, and

(b) adopt procedures suitable to the circumstances of the particular case, avoiding unnecessary delay or expense, so as to provide a fair means for the resolution of the matters falling to be determined.

(2) The tribunal shall comply with that general duty in conducting the arbitral proceedings, in its decisions on matters of procedure and evidence and in the exercise of all other powers conferred on it.

Procedural and evidential matters

34.—(1) It shall be for the tribunal to decide all procedural and evidential matters, subject to the right of the parties to agree any matter.

(2) Procedural and evidential matters include—

(a) when and where any part of the proceedings is to be held;

(b) the language or languages to be used in the proceedings and whether translations of any relevant documents are to be supplied;

(c) whether any and if so what form of written statements of claim and defence are to be used, when these should be supplied and the extent to which such statements can be later amended;

(d) whether any and if so which documents or classes of documents should be disclosed between and produced by the parties and at what stage;

(e) whether any and if so what questions should be put to and answered by the respective parties and when and in what form this should be done;

(f) whether to apply strict rules of evidence (or any other rules) as to the admissibility, relevance or weight of any material (oral, written or other) sought to be tendered on any matters of fact or opinion, and the time, manner and form in which such material should be exchanged and presented;

(g) whether and to what extent the tribunal should itself take the initiative in ascertaining the facts and the law;

(h) whether and to what extent there should be oral or written evidence or submissions.

(3) The tribunal may fix the time within which any directions given by it are to be complied with, and may if it thinks fit extend the time so fixed (whether or not it has expired).

Consolidation of proceedings and concurrent hearings

35.—(1) The parties are free to agree—

(a) that the arbitral proceedings shall be consolidated with other arbitral proceedings, or

(b) that concurrent hearings shall be held,

on such terms as may be agreed.

(2) Unless the parties agree to confer such power on the tribunal, the tribunal has no power to order consolidation of proceedings or concurrent hearings.

Legal or other representation

36. Unless otherwise agreed by the parties, a party to arbitral proceedings may be represented in the proceedings by a lawyer or other person chosen by him.

Power to appoint experts, legal advisers or assessors

37.—(1) Unless otherwise agreed by the parties—

(a) the tribunal may—

(i) appoint experts or legal advisers to report to it and the parties, or

(ii) appoint assessors to assist it on technical matters,

and may allow any such expert, legal adviser or assessor to attend the proceedings; and

(b) the parties shall be given a reasonable opportunity to comment on any information, opinion or advice offered by any such person.

(2) The fees and expenses of an expert, legal adviser or assessor appointed by the tribunal for which the arbitrators are liable are expenses of the arbitrators for the purposes of this Part.

General powers exercisable by the tribunal

38.—(1) The parties are free to agree on the powers exercisable by the arbitral tribunal for the purposes of and in relation to the proceedings.

(2) Unless otherwise agreed by the parties the tribunal has the following powers.

(3) The tribunal may order a claimant to provide security for the costs of the arbitration.

This power shall not be exercised on the ground that the claimant is—

(a) an individual ordinarily resident outside the United Kingdom, or

(b) a corporation or association incorporated or formed under the law of a country outside the United Kingdom, or whose central management and control is exercised outside the United Kingdom.

(4) The tribunal may give directions in relation to any property which is the subject of the proceedings or as to which any question arises in the proceedings, and which is owned by or is in the possession of a party to the proceedings—

(a) for the inspection, photographing, preservation, custody or detention of the property by the tribunal, an expert or a party, or

(b) ordering that samples be taken from, or any observation be made of or experiment conducted upon, the property.

(5) The tribunal may direct that a party or witness shall be examined on oath or affirmation, and may for that purpose administer any necessary oath or take any necessary affirmation.

(6) The tribunal may give directions to a party for the preservation for the purposes of the proceedings of any evidence in his custody or control.

Power to make provisional awards

39.—(1) The parties are free to agree that the tribunal shall have power to order on a provisional basis any relief which it would have power to grant in a final award.

(2) This includes, for instance, making—

(a) a provisional order for the payment of money or the disposition of property as between the parties, or

(b) an order to make an interim payment on account of the costs of the arbitration.

(3) Any such order shall be subject to the tribunal's final adjudication and the tribunal's final award, on the merits or as to costs, shall take account of any such order.

(4) Unless the parties agree to confer such power on the tribunal, the tribunal has no such power.

This does not affect its powers under section 47 (awards on different issues, &c.).

General duty of parties

40.—(1) The parties shall do all things necessary for the proper and expeditious conduct of the arbitral proceedings.

(2) This includes—

(a) complying without delay with any determination of the tribunal as to procedural or evidential matters, or with any order or directions of the tribunal, and

(b) where appropriate, taking without delay any necessary steps to obtain a decision of the court on a preliminary question of jurisdiction or law (see sections 32 and 45).

Powers of tribunal in case of party's default

41.—(1) The parties are free to agree on the powers of the tribunal in case of a party's failure to do something necessary for the proper and expeditious conduct of the arbitration.

(2) Unless otherwise agreed by the parties, the following provisions apply.

(3) If the tribunal is satisfied that there has been inordinate and inexcusable delay on the part of the claimant in pursuing his claim and that the delay—

(a) gives rise, or is likely to give rise, to a substantial risk that it is not possible to have a fair resolution of the issues in that claim, or
(b) has caused, or is likely to cause, serious prejudice to the respondent,

the tribunal may make an award dismissing the claim.

(4) If without showing sufficient cause a party—

(a) fails to attend or be represented at an oral hearing of which due notice was given, or
(b) where matters are to be dealt with in writing, fails after due notice to submit written evidence or make written submissions,

the tribunal may continue the proceedings in the absence of that party or, as the case may be, without any written evidence or submissions on his behalf, and may make an award on the basis of the evidence before it.

(5) If without showing sufficient cause a party fails to comply with any order or directions of the tribunal, the tribunal may make a peremptory order to the same effect, prescribing such time for compliance with it as the tribunal considers appropriate.

(6) If a claimant fails to comply with a peremptory order of the tribunal to provide security for costs, the tribunal may make an award dismissing his claim.

(7) If a party fails to comply with any other kind of peremptory order, then, without prejudice to section 42 (enforcement by court of tribunal's peremptory orders), the tribunal may do any of the following—

(a) direct that the party in default shall not be entitled to rely upon any allegation or material which was the subject matter of the order;
(b) draw such adverse inferences from the act of non-compliance as the circumstances justify;
(c) proceed to an award on the basis of such materials as have been properly provided to it;
(d) make such order as it thinks fit as to the payment of costs of the arbitration incurred in consequence of the non-compliance.

POWERS OF COURT IN RELATION TO ARBITRAL PROCEEDINGS

Enforcement of peremptory orders of tribunal

42.—(1) Unless otherwise agreed by the parties, the court may make an order requiring a party to comply with a peremptory order made by the tribunal.

(2) An application for an order under this section may be made—

(a) by the tribunal (upon notice to the parties),

(b) by a party to the arbitral proceedings with the permission of the tribunal (and upon notice to the other parties), or

(c) where the parties have agreed that the powers of the court under this section shall be available.

(3) The court shall not act unless it is satisfied that the applicant has exhausted any available arbitral process in respect of failure to comply with the tribunal's order.

(4) No order shall be made under this section unless the court is satisfied that the person to whom the tribunal's order was directed has failed to comply with it within the time prescribed in the order or, if no time was prescribed, within a reasonable time.

(5) The leave of the court is required for any appeal from a decision of the court under this section.

Securing the attendance of witnesses

43.—(1) A party to arbitral proceedings may use the same court procedures as are available in relation to legal proceedings to secure the attendance before the tribunal of a witness in order to give oral testimony or to produce documents or other material evidence.

(2) This may only be done with the permission of the tribunal or the agreement of the other parties.

(3) The court procedures may only be used if—

(a) the witness is in the United Kingdom, and

(b) the arbitral proceedings are being conducted in England and Wales or, as the case may be, Northern Ireland.

(4) A person shall not be compelled by virtue of this section to produce any document or other material evidence which he could not be compelled to produce in legal proceedings.

Court powers exercisable in support of arbitral proceedings

44.—(1) Unless otherwise agreed by the parties, the court has for the purposes of and in relation to arbitral proceedings the same power of making orders about the matters listed below as it has for the purposes of and in relation to legal proceedings.

(2) Those matters are—

(a) the taking of the evidence of witnesses;

(b) the preservation of evidence;

(c) making orders relating to property which is the subject of the proceedings or as to which any question arises in the proceedings—

(i) for the inspection, photographing, preservation, custody or detention of the property, or

(ii) ordering that samples be taken from, or any observation be made of or experiment conducted upon, the property;

and for that purpose authorising any person to enter any premises in the possession or control of a party to the arbitration;

(d) the sale of any goods the subject of the proceedings;

(e) the granting of an interim injunction or the appointment of a receiver.

(3) If the case is one of urgency, the court may, on the application of a party or proposed party to the arbitral proceedings, make such orders as it thinks necessary for the purpose of preserving evidence or assets.

(4) If the case is not one of urgency, the court shall act only on the application of a party to the arbitral proceedings (upon notice to the other parties and to the tribunal) made with the permission of the tribunal or the agreement in writing of the other parties.

(5) In any case the court shall act only if or to the extent that the arbitral tribunal, and any arbitral or other institution or person vested by the parties with power in that regard, has no power or is unable for the time being to act effectively.

(6) If the court so orders, an order made by it under this section shall cease to have effect in whole or in part on the order of the tribunal or of any such arbitral or other institution or person having power to act in relation to the subject-matter of the order.

(7) The leave of the court is required for any appeal from a decision of the court under this section.

Determination of preliminary point of law

45.—(1) Unless otherwise agreed by the parties, the court may on the application of a party to arbitral proceedings (upon notice to the other parties) determine any question of law arising in the course of the proceedings which the court is satisfied substantially affects the rights of one or more of the parties.

An agreement to dispense with reasons for the tribunal's award shall be considered an agreement to exclude the court's jurisdiction under this section.

(2) An application under this section shall not be considered unless—

(a) it is made with the agreement of all the other parties to the proceedings, or

(b) it is made with the permission of the tribunal and the court is satisfied—

(i) that the determination of the question is likely to produce substantial savings in costs, and

(ii) that the application was made without delay.

(3) The application shall identify the question of law to be determined and, unless made with the agreement of all the other parties to the proceedings, shall state the grounds on which it is said that the question should be decided by the court.

(4) Unless otherwise agreed by the parties, the arbitral tribunal may continue the arbitral proceedings and make an award while an application to the court under this section is pending.

(5) Unless the court gives leave, no appeal lies from a decision of the court whether the conditions specified in subsection (2) are met.

(6) The decision of the court on the question of law shall be treated as a judgement of the court for the purposes of an appeal.

But no appeal lies without the leave of the court which shall not be given unless the court considers that the question is one of general importance, or is one which for some other special reason should be considered by the Court of Appeal.

THE AWARD

Rules applicable to substance of dispute

46.—(1) The arbitral tribunal shall decide the dispute—

(a) in accordance with the law chosen by the parties as applicable to the substance of the dispute, or

(b) if the parties so agree, in accordance with such other considerations as are agreed by them or determined by the tribunal.

(2) For this purpose the choice of the laws of a country shall be understood to refer to the substantive laws of that country and not its conflict of laws rules.

(3) If or to the extent that there is no such choice or agreement, the tribunal shall apply the law determined by the conflict of laws rules which it considers applicable.

Awards on different issues, &c.

47.—(1) Unless otherwise agreed by the parties, the tribunal may make more than one award at different times on different aspects of the matters to be determined.

(2) The tribunal may, in particular, make an award relating—

(a) to an issue affecting the whole claim, or

(b) to a part only of the claims or cross-claims submitted to it for decision.

(3) If the tribunal does so, it shall specify in its award the issue, or the claim or part of a claim, which is the subject matter of the award.

Remedies

48.—(1) The parties are free to agree on the powers exercisable by the arbitral tribunal as regards remedies.

(2) Unless otherwise agreed by the parties, the tribunal has the following powers.

(3) The tribunal may make a declaration as to any matter to be determined in the proceedings.

(4) The tribunal may order the payment of a sum of money, in any currency.

(5) The tribunal has the same powers as the court—

(a) to order a party to do or refrain from doing anything;

(b) to order specific performance of a contract (other than a contract relating to land);

(c) to order the rectification, setting aside or cancellation of a deed or other document.

Interest

49.—(1) The parties are free to agree on the powers of the tribunal as regards the award of interest.

(2) Unless otherwise agreed by the parties the following provisions apply.

(3) The tribunal may award simple or compound interest from such dates, at such rates and with such rests as it considers meets the justice of the case—

(a) on the whole or part of any amount awarded by the tribunal, in respect of any period up to the date of the award;

(b) on the whole or part of any amount claimed in the arbitration and outstanding at the commencement of the arbitral proceedings but paid before the award was made, in respect of any period up to the date of payment.

(4) The tribunal may award simple or compound interest from the date of the award (or any later date) until payment, at such rates and with such rests as it considers meets the justice of the case, on the outstanding amount of any award (including any award of interest under subsection (3) and any award as to costs).

(5) References in this section to an amount awarded by the tribunal include an amount payable in consequence of a declaratory award by the tribunal.

(6) The above provisions do not affect any other power of the tribunal to award interest.

Extension of time for making award

50.—(1) Where the time for making an award is limited by or in pursuance of the arbitration agreement, then, unless otherwise agreed by the parties, the court may in accordance with the following provisions by order extend that time.

(2) An application for an order under this section may be made—

(a) by the tribunal (upon notice to the parties), or

(b) by any party to the proceedings (upon notice to the tribunal and the other parties),

but only after exhausting any available arbitral process for obtaining an extension of time.

(3) The court shall only make an order if satisfied that a substantial injustice would otherwise be done.

(4) The court may extend the time for such period and on such terms as it thinks fit, and may do so whether or not the time previously fixed (by or under the agreement or by a previous order) has expired.

(5) The leave of the court is required for any appeal from a decision of the court under this section.

Settlement

51.—(1) If during arbitral proceedings the parties settle the dispute, the following provisions apply unless otherwise agreed by the parties.

(2) The tribunal shall terminate the substantive proceedings and, if so requested by the parties and not objected to by the tribunal, shall record the settlement in the form of an agreed award.

(3) An agreed award shall state that it is an award of the tribunal and shall have the same status and effect as any other award on the merits of the case.

(4) The following provisions of this Part relating to awards (sections 52 to 58) apply to an agreed award.

(5) Unless the parties have also settled the matter of the payment of the costs of the arbitration, the provisions of this Part relating to costs (sections 59 to 65) continue to apply.

Form of award

52.—(1) The parties are free to agree on the form of an award.

(2) If or to the extent that there is no such agreement, the following provisions apply.

(3) The award shall be in writing signed by all the arbitrators or all those assenting to the award.

(4) The award shall contain the reasons for the award unless it is an agreed award or the parties have agreed to dispense with reasons.

(5) The award shall state the seat of the arbitration and the date when the award is made.

Place where award treated as made

53. Unless otherwise agreed by the parties, where the seat of the arbitration is in England and Wales or Northern Ireland, any award in the proceedings shall be treated as made there, regardless of where it was signed, despatched or delivered to any of the parties.

Date of award

54.—(1) Unless otherwise agreed by the parties, the tribunal may decide what is to be taken to be the date on which the award was made.

(2) In the absence of any such decision, the date of the award shall be taken to be the date on which it is signed by the arbitrator or, where more than one arbitrator signs the award, by the last of them.

Notification of award

55.—(1) The parties are free to agree on the requirements as to notification of the award to the parties.

(2) If there is no such agreement, the award shall be notified to the parties by service on them of copies of the award, which shall be done without delay after the award is made.

(3) Nothing in this section affects section 56 (power to withhold award in case of non-payment).

Power to withhold award in case of non-payment

56.—(1) The tribunal may refuse to deliver an award to the parties except upon full payment of the fees and expenses of the arbitrators.

(2) If the tribunal refuses on that ground to deliver an award, a party to the arbitral proceedings may (upon notice to the other parties and the tribunal) apply to the court, which may order that—

(a) the tribunal shall deliver the award on the payment into court by the applicant of the fees and expenses demanded, or such lesser amount as the court may specify,

(b) the amount of the fees and expenses properly payable shall be determined by such means and upon such terms as the court may direct, and

(c) out of the money paid into court there shall be paid out such fees and expenses as may be found to be properly payable and the balance of the money (if any) shall be paid out to the applicant.

(3) For this purpose the amount of fees and expenses properly

payable is the amount the applicant is liable to pay under section 28 or any agreement relating to the payment of the arbitrators.

(4) No application to the court may be made where there is any available arbitral process for appeal or review of the amount of the fees or expenses demanded.

(5) References in this section to arbitrators include an arbitrator who has ceased to act and an umpire who has not replaced the other arbitrators.

(6) The above provisions of this section also apply in relation to any arbitral or other institution or person vested by the parties with powers in relation to the delivery of the tribunal's award.

As they so apply, the references to the fees and expenses of the arbitrators shall be construed as including the fees and expenses of that institution or person.

(7) The leave of the court is required for any appeal from a decision of the court under this section.

(8) Nothing in this section shall be construed as excluding an application under section 28 where payment has been made to the arbitrators in order to obtain the award.

Correction of award or additional award

57.—(1) The parties are free to agree on the powers of the tribunal to correct an award or make an additional award.

(2) If or to the extent there is no such agreement, the following provisions apply.

(3) The tribunal may on its own initiative or on the application of a party—

(a) correct an award so as to remove any clerical mistake or error arising from an accidental slip or omission or clarify or remove any ambiguity in the award, or

(b) make an additional award in respect of any claim (including a claim for interest or costs) which was presented to the tribunal but was not dealt with in the award.

These powers shall not be exercised without first affording the other parties a reasonable opportunity to make representations to the tribunal.

(4) Any application for the exercise of those powers must be made within 28 days of the date of the award or such longer period as the parties may agree.

(5) Any correction of an award shall be made within 28 days of the

date the application was received by the tribunal or, where the correction is made by the tribunal on its own initiative, within 28 days of the date of the award or, in either case, such longer period as the parties may agree.

(6) Any additional award shall be made within 56 days of the date of the original award or such longer period as the parties may agree.

(7) Any correction of an award shall form part of the award.

Effect of award

58.—(1) Unless otherwise agreed by the parties, an award made by the tribunal pursuant to an arbitration agreement is final and binding both on the parties and on any persons claiming through or under them.

(2) This does not affect the right of a person to challenge the award by any available arbitral process of appeal or review or in accordance with the provisions of this Part.

COSTS OF THE ARBITRATION

Costs of the arbitration

59.—(1) References in this Part to the costs of the arbitration are to—

(a) the arbitrators' fees and expenses,

(b) the fees and expenses of any arbitral institution concerned, and

(c) the legal or other costs of the parties.

(2) Any such reference includes the costs of or incidental to any proceedings to determine the amount of the recoverable costs of the arbitration (see section 63).

Agreement to pay costs in any event

60. An agreement which has the effect that a party is to pay the whole or part of the costs of the arbitration in any event is only valid if made after the dispute in question has arisen.

Award of costs

61.—(1) The tribunal may make an award allocating the costs of the arbitration as between the parties, subject to any agreement of the parties.

(2) Unless the parties otherwise agree, the tribunal shall award costs on the general principle that costs should follow the event except where it appears to the tribunal that in the circumstances this is not appropriate in relation to the whole or part of the costs.

Effect of agreement or award about costs

62. Unless the parties otherwise agree, any obligation under an agreement between them as to how the costs of the arbitration are to be borne, or under an award allocating the costs of the arbitration, extends only to such costs as are recoverable.

The recoverable costs of the arbitration

63.—(1) The parties are free to agree what costs of the arbitration are recoverable.

(2) If or to the extent there is no such agreement, the following provisions apply.

(3) The tribunal may determine by award the recoverable costs of the arbitration on such basis as it thinks fit.

If it does so, it shall specify—

(a) the basis on which it has acted, and

(b) the items of recoverable costs and the amount referable to each.

(4) If the tribunal does not determine the recoverable costs of the arbitration, any party to the arbitral proceedings may apply to the court (upon notice to the other parties) which may—

(a) determine the recoverable costs of the arbitration on such basis as it thinks fit, or

(b) order that they shall be determined by such means and upon such terms as it may specify.

(5) Unless the tribunal or the court determines otherwise—

(a) the recoverable costs of the arbitration shall be determined on the basis that there shall be allowed a reasonable amount in respect of all costs reasonably incurred, and

(b) any doubt as to whether costs were reasonably incurred or were reasonable in amount shall be resolved in favour of the paying party.

(6) The above provisions have effect subject to section 64 (recoverable fees and expenses of arbitrators).

(7) Nothing in this section affects any right of the arbitrators, any

expert, legal adviser or assessor appointed by the tribunal, or any arbitral institution, to payment of their fees and expenses.

Recoverable fees and expenses of arbitrators

64.—(1) Unless otherwise agreed by the parties, the recoverable costs of the arbitration shall include in respect of the fees and expenses of the arbitrators only such reasonable fees and expenses as are appropriate in the circumstances.

(2) If there is any question as to what reasonable fees and expenses are appropriate in the circumstances, and the matter is not already before the court on an application under section 63(4), the court may on the application of any party (upon notice to the other parties)—

(a) determine the matter, or

(b) order that it be determined by such means and upon such terms as the court may specify.

(3) Subsection (1) has effect subject to any order of the court under section 24(4) or 25(3)(b) (order as to entitlement to fees or expenses in case of removal or resignation of arbitrator).

(4) Nothing in this section affects any right of the arbitrator to payment of his fees and expenses.

Power to limit recoverable costs

65.—(1) Unless otherwise agreed by the parties, the tribunal may direct that the recoverable costs of the arbitration, or of any part of the arbitral proceedings, shall be limited to a specified amount.

(2) Any direction may be made or varied at any stage, but this must be done sufficiently in advance of the incurring of costs to which it relates, or the taking of any steps in the proceedings which may be affected by it, for the limit to be taken into account.

POWERS OF THE COURT IN RELATION TO AWARD

Enforcement of the award

66.—(1) An award made by the tribunal pursuant to an arbitration agreement may, by leave of the court, be enforced in the same manner as a judgment or order of the court to the same effect.

(2) Where leave is so given, judgment may be entered in terms of the award.

(3) Leave to enforce an award shall not be given where, or to the extent that, the person against whom it is sought to be enforced shows that the tribunal lacked substantive jurisdiction to make the award.

The right to raise such an objection may have been lost (see section 73).

(4) Nothing in this section affects the recognition or enforcement of an award under any other enactment or rule of law, in particular under Part II of the Arbitration Act 1950 (enforcement of awards under Geneva Convention) or the provisions of Part III of this Act relating to the recognition and enforcement of awards under the New York Convention or by an action on the award.

Challenging the award: substantive jurisdiction

67.—(1) A party to arbitral proceedings may (upon notice to the other parties and to the tribunal) apply to the court—

(a) challenging any award of the arbitral tribunal as to its substantive jurisdiction; or

(b) for an order declaring an award made by the tribunal on the merits to be of no effect, in whole or in part, because the tribunal did not have substantive jurisdiction.

A party may lose the right to object (see section 73) and the right to apply is subject to the restrictions in section 70(2) and (3).

(2) The arbitral tribunal may continue the arbitral proceedings and make a further award while an application to the court under this section is pending in relation to an award as to jurisdiction.

(3) On an application under this section challenging an award of the arbitral tribunal as to its substantive jurisdiction, the court may by order—

(a) confirm the award,

(b) vary the award, or

(c) set aside the award in whole or in part.

(4) The leave of the court is required for any appeal from a decision of the court under this section.

Challenging the award: serious irregularity

68.—(1) A party to arbitral proceedings may (upon notice to the other parties and to the tribunal) apply to the court challenging an award in the proceedings on the ground of serious irregularity affecting the tribunal, the proceedings or the award.

A party may lose the right to object (see section 73) and the right to apply is subject to the restrictions in section 70(2) and (3).

(2) Serious irregularity means an irregularity of one or more of the following kinds which the court considers has caused or will cause substantial injustice to the applicant—

(a) failure by the tribunal to comply with section 33 (general duty of tribunal);
(b) the tribunal exceeding its powers (otherwise than by exceeding its substantive jurisdiction: see section 67);
(c) failure by the tribunal to conduct the proceedings in accordance with the procedure agreed by the parties;
(d) failure by the tribunal to deal with all the issues that were put to it;
(e) any arbitral or other institution or person vested by the parties with powers in relation to the proceedings or the award exceeding its powers;
(f) uncertainty or ambiguity as to the effect of the award;
(g) the award being obtained by fraud or the award or the way in which it was procured being contrary to public policy;
(h) failure to comply with the requirements as to the form of the award or
(i) any irregularity in the conduct of the proceedings or in the award which is admitted by the tribunal or by any arbitral or other institution or person vested by the parties with powers in relation to the proceedings or the award.

(3) If there is shown to be serious irregularity affecting the tribunal, the proceedings or the award, the court may—

(a) remit the award to the tribunal, in whole or in part, for reconsideration,
(b) set the award aside in whole or in part, or
(c) declare the award to be of no effect, in whole or in part.

The court shall not exercise its power to set aside or to declare an award to be of no effect, in whole or in part, unless it is satisfied that it would be inappropriate to remit the matters in question to the tribunal for reconsideration.

(4) The leave of the court is required for any appeal from a decision of the court under this section.

Appeal on point of law

69.—(1) Unless otherwise agreed by the parties, a party to arbitral proceedings may (upon notice to the other parties and to the tribunal) appeal to the court on a question of law arising out of an award made in the proceedings.

An agreement to dispense with reasons for the tribunal's award shall be considered an agreement to exclude the court's jurisdiction under this section.

(2) An appeal shall not be brought under this section except—

(a) with the agreement of all the other parties to the proceedings, or

(b) with the leave of the court.

The right to appeal is also subject to the restrictions in section 70(2) and (3).

(3) Leave to appeal shall be given only if the court is satisfied—

(a) that the determination of the question will substantially affect the rights of one or more of the parties,

(b) that the question is one which the tribunal was asked to determine,

(c) that, on the basis of the findings of fact in the award—

(i) the decision of the tribunal on the question is obviously wrong, or

(ii) the question is one of general public importance and the decision of the tribunal is at least open to serious doubt, and

(d) that, despite the agreement of the parties to resolve the matter by arbitration, it is just and proper in all the circumstances for the court to determine the question.

(4) An application for leave to appeal under this section shall identify the question of law to be determined and state the grounds on which it is alleged that leave to appeal should be granted.

(5) The court shall determine an application for leave to appeal under this section without a hearing unless it appears to the court that a hearing is required.

(6) The leave of the court is required for any appeal from a decision of the court under this section to grant or refuse leave to appeal.

(7) On an appeal under this section the court may by order—

(a) confirm the award,

(b) vary the award,

(c) remit the award to the tribunal, in whole or in part, for reconsideration in the light of the court's determination, or

(d) set aside the award in whole or in part.

The court shall not exercise its power to set aside an award, in whole or in part, unless it is satisfied that it would be inappropriate to remit the matters in question to the tribunal for reconsideration.

(8) The decision of the court on an appeal under this section shall be treated as a judgment of the court for the purposes of a further appeal.

But no such appeal lies without the leave of the court which shall not be given unless the court considers that the question is one of general importance or is one which for some other special reason should be considered by the Court of Appeal.

Challenge or appeal: supplementary provisions

70.—(1) The following provisions apply to an application or appeal under section 67, 68 or 69.

(2) An application or appeal may not be brought if the applicant or appellant has not first exhausted—

(a) any available arbitral process of appeal or review, and

(b) any available recourse under section 57 (correction of award or additional award).

(3) Any application or appeal must be brought within 28 days of the date of the award or, if there has been any arbitral process of appeal or review, of the date when the applicant or appellant was notified of the result of that process.

(4) If on an application or appeal it appears to the court that the award—

(a) does not contain the tribunal's reasons, or

(b) does not set out the tribunal's reasons in sufficient detail to enable the court properly to consider the application or appeal,

the court may order the tribunal to state the reasons for its award in sufficient detail for that purpose.

(5) Where the court makes an order under subsection (4), it may make such further order as it thinks fit with respect to any additional costs of the arbitration resulting from its order.

(6) The court may order the applicant or appellant to provide security for the costs of the application or appeal, and may direct that

the application or appeal be dismissed if the order is not complied with.

The power to order security for costs shall not be exercised on the ground that the applicant or appellant is—

(a) an individual ordinarily resident outside the United Kingdom, or

(b) a corporation or association incorporated or formed under the law of a country outside the United Kingdom, or whose central management and control is exercised outside the United Kingdom.

(7) The court may order that any money payable under the award shall be brought into court or otherwise secured pending the determination of the application or appeal, and may direct that the application or appeal be dismissed if the order is not complied with.

(8) The court may grant leave to appeal subject to conditions to the same or similar effect as an order under subsection (6) or (7).

This does not affect the general discretion of the court to grant leave subject to conditions.

Challenge or appeal: effect of order of court

71.—(1) The following provisions have effect where the court makes an order under section 67, 68 or 69 with respect to an award.

(2) Where the award is varied, the variation has effect as part of the tribunal's award.

(3) Where the award is remitted to the tribunal, in whole or in part, for reconsideration, the tribunal shall make a fresh award in respect of the matters remitted within three months of the date of the order for remission or such longer or shorter period as the court may direct.

(4) Where the award is set aside or declared to be of no effect, in whole or in part, the court may also order that any provision that an award is a condition precedent to the bringing of legal proceedings in respect of a matter to which the arbitration agreement applies, is of no effect as regards the subject matter of the award or, as the case may be, the relevant part of the award.

MISCELLANEOUS

Saving for rights of person who takes no part in proceedings

72.—(1) A person alleged to be a party to arbitral proceedings but who takes no part in the proceedings may question—

(a) whether there is a valid arbitration agreement,
(b) whether the tribunal is properly constituted, or
(c) what matters have been submitted to arbitration in accordance with the arbitration agreement,

by proceedings in the court for a declaration or injunction or other appropriate relief.

(2) He also has the same right as a party to the arbitral proceedings to challenge an award—

(a) by an application under section 67 on the ground of lack of substantive jurisdiction in relation to him, or
(b) by an application under section 68 on the ground of serious irregularity (within the meaning of that section) affecting him;

and section 70(2) (duty to exhaust arbitral procedures) does not apply in this case.

Loss of right to object

73.—(1) If a party to arbitral proceedings takes part, or continues to take part, in the proceedings without making, either forthwith or within such time as is allowed by the arbitration agreement or the tribunal or by any Provision of this Part, any objection—

(a) that the tribunal lacks substantive jurisdiction,
(b) that the proceedings have been improperly conducted,
(c) that there has been a failure to comply with the arbitration agreement or with any provision of this Part, or
(d) that there has been any other irregularity affecting the tribunal or the proceedings,

he may not raise that objection later, before the tribunal or the court, unless he shows that, at the time he took part or continued to take part in the proceedings, he did not know and could not with reasonable diligence have discovered the grounds for the objection.

(2) Where the arbitral tribunal rules that it has substantive jurisdiction and a party to arbitral proceedings who could have questioned that ruling—

(a) by any available arbitral process of appeal or review, or

(b) by challenging the award,

does not do so, or does not do so within the time allowed by the arbitration agreement or any provision of this Part, he may not object later to the tribunal's substantive jurisdiction on any ground which was the subject of that ruling.

Immunity of arbitral institutions, &c.

74.—(1) An arbitral or other institution or person designated or requested by the parties to appoint or nominate an arbitrator is not liable for anything done or omitted in the discharge or purported discharge of that function unless the act or omission is shown to have been in bad faith.

(2) An arbitral or other institution or person by whom an arbitrator is appointed or nominated is not liable, by reason of having appointed or nominated him, for anything done or omitted by the arbitrator (or his employees or agents) in the discharge or purported discharge of his functions as arbitrator.

(3) The above provisions apply to an employee or agent of an arbitral or other institution or person as they apply to the institution or person himself.

Charge to secure payment of solicitors' costs

75. The powers of the court to make declarations and orders under section 73 of the Solicitors Act 1974 or Article 71H of the Solicitors (Northern Ireland) Order 1976 (power to charge property recovered in the proceedings with the payment of solicitors' costs) may be exercised in relation to arbitral proceedings as if those proceedings were proceedings in the court.

SUPPLEMENTARY

Service of notices, &c.

76.—(1) The parties are free to agree on the manner of service of any notice or other document required or authorised to be given or served in pursuance of the arbitration agreement or for the purpose of the arbitral proceedings.

(2) If or to the extent that there is no such agreement the following provisions apply.

(3) A notice or other document may be served on a person by any effective means.

(4) If a notice or other document is addressed, pre-paid and delivered by post—

(a) to the addressee's last known principal residence or, if he is or has been carrying on a trade, profession or business, his last known principal business address, or

(b) where the addressee is a body corporate, to the body's registered or principal office,

it shall be treated as effectively served.

(5) This section does not apply to the service of documents for the purposes of legal proceedings, for which provision is made by rules of court.

(6) References in this Part to a notice or other document include any form of communication in writing and references to giving or serving a notice or other document shall be served accordingly.

Powers of court in relation to service of documents

77.—(1) This section applies where service of a document on a person in the manner agreed by the parties, or in accordance with the provisions of section 76 having effect in default of agreement, is not reasonably practicable.

(2) Unless otherwise agreed by the parties, the court may make such order as it thinks fit—

(a) for service in such manner as the court may direct, or

(b) dispensing with service of the document.

(3) Any party to the arbitration agreement may apply for an order, but only after exhausting any available arbitral process for resolving the matter.

(4) The leave of the court is required for any appeal from a decision of the court under this section.

Reckoning periods of time

78.—(1) The parties are free to agree on the method of reckoning periods of time for the purposes of any provision agreed by them or any provision of this Part having effect in default of such agreement.

(2) If or to the extent there is no such agreement, periods of time shall be reckoned in accordance with the following provisions.

(3) Where the act is required to be done within a specified period after or from a specified date, the period begins immediately after that date.

(4) Where the act is required to be done a specified number of clear days after a specified date, at least that number of days must intervene between the day on which the act is done and that date.

(5) Where the period is a period of seven days or less which would include a Saturday, Sunday or a public holiday in the place where anything which has to be done within the period falls to be done, that day shall be excluded.

In relation to England and Wales or Northern Ireland, a "public holiday" means Christmas Day, Good Friday or a day which under the Banking and Financial Dealings Act 1971 is a bank holiday.

Power of court to extend time limits relating to arbitral proceedings

79.—(1) Unless the parties otherwise agree, the court may by order extend any time limit agreed by them in relation to any matter relating to the arbitral proceedings or specified in any provision of this Part having effect in default of such agreement.

This section does not apply to a time limit to which section 12 applies (power of court to extend time for beginning arbitral proceedings, &c.).

(2) An application for an order may be made—

(a) by any party to the arbitral proceedings (upon notice to the other parties and to the tribunal), or

(b) by the arbitral tribunal (upon notice to the parties).

(3) The court shall not exercise its power to extend a time limit unless it is satisfied—

(a) that any available recourse to the tribunal, or to any arbitral or other institution or person vested by the parties with power in that regard, has first been exhausted, and

(b) that a substantial injustice would otherwise be done.

(4) The court's power under this section may be exercised whether or not the time has already expired.

(5) An order under this section may be made on such terms as the court thinks fit.

(6) The leave of the court is required for any appeal from a decision of the court under this section.

Notice and other requirements in connection with legal proceedings

80.—(1) References in this Part to an application, appeal or other step in relation to legal proceedings being taken "upon notice" to the other parties to the arbitral proceedings, or to the tribunal, are to such notice of the originating process as is required by rules of court and do not impose any separate requirement.

(2) Rules of court shall be made—

(a) requiring such notice to be given as indicated by any provision of this Part, and

(b) as to the manner, form and content of any such notice.

(3) Subject to any provision made by rules of court, a requirement to give notice to the tribunal of legal proceedings shall be construed—

(a) if there is more than one arbitrator, as a requirement to give notice to each of them; and

(b) if the tribunal is not fully constituted, as a requirement to give notice to any arbitrator who has been appointed.

(4) References in this Part to making an application or appeal to the court within a specified period are to the issue within that period of the appropriate originating process in accordance with rules of court.

(5) Where any provision of this Part requires an application or appeal to be made to the court within a specified time, the rules of court relating to the reckoning of periods, the extending or abridging of periods, and the consequences of not taking a step within the period prescribed by the rules, apply in relation to that requirement.

(6) Provision may be made by rules of court amending the provisions of this Part—

(a) with respect to the time within which any application or appeal to the court must be made,

(b) so as to keep any provision made by this Part in relation to arbitral proceedings in step with the corresponding provision of rules of court applying in relation to proceedings in the court, or

(c) so as to keep any provision made by this Part in relation to legal proceedings in step with the corresponding provision of rules of court applying generally in relation to proceedings in the court.

(7) Nothing in this section affects the generality of the power to make rules of court.

Saving for certain matters governed by common law

81.—(1) Nothing in this Part shall be construed as excluding the operation of any rule of law consistent with the provisions of this Part, in particular, any rule of law as to—

(a) matters which are not capable of settlement by arbitration;

(b) the effect of an oral arbitration agreement; or

(c) the refusal of recognition or enforcement of an arbitral award on grounds of public policy.

(2) Nothing in this Act shall be construed as reviving any jurisdiction of the court to set aside or remit an award on the ground of errors of fact or law on the face of the award.

Minor definitions

82.—(1) In this Part—

"arbitrator", unless the context otherwise requires, includes an umpire;

"available arbitral process", in relation to any matter, includes any process of appeal to or review by an arbitral or other institution or person vested by the parties with powers in relation to that matter;

"claimant", unless the context otherwise requires, includes a counterclaimant, and related expressions shall be construed accordingly;

"dispute" includes any difference;

"enactment" includes an enactment contained in Northern Ireland legislation;

"legal proceedings" means civil proceedings in the High Court or a county court;

"peremptory order" means an order made under section 41(5) or made in exercise of any corresponding power conferred by the parties;

"premises" includes land, buildings, moveable structures, vehicles, vessels, aircraft and hovercraft;

"question of law" means—

(a) for a court in England and Wales, a question of the law of England and Wales, and

(b) for a court in Northern Ireland, a question of the law of Northern Ireland;

"substantive jurisdiction", in relation to an arbitral tribunal, refers to the matters specified in section 30(1)(a) to (c), and references to the tribunal exceeding its substantive jurisdiction shall be construed accordingly.

(2) References in this Part to a party to an arbitration agreement include any person claiming under or through a party to the agreement.

Index of defined expressions: Part I

83. In this Part the expressions listed below are defined or otherwise explained by the provisions indicated—

agreement, agree and agreed	section 5(1)
agreement in writing	section 5(2) to (5)
arbitration agreement	sections 6 and 5(1)
arbitrator	section 82(1)
available arbitral process	section 82(1)
claimant	section 82(1)
commencement (in relation to arbitral proceedings)	section 14
costs of the arbitration	section 59
the court	section 105
dispute	section 82(1)
enactment	section 82(1)
legal proceedings	section 82(1)
Limitation Acts	section 13(4)
notice (or other document)	section 76(6)
party—	
—in relation to an arbitration agreement	section 82(2)
—where section 106(2) or (3) applies	section 106(4)
peremptory order	section 82(1) (and see section 41(5))
premises	section 82(1)
question of law	section 82(1)
recoverable costs	sections 63 and 64
seat of the arbitration	section 3
serve and service (of notice or other document)	section 76(6)
substantive jurisdiction (in relation to an arbitral tribunal)	section 82(1) (and see section 30(1) (a) to (c))

upon notice (to the parties or the tribunal)	section 80
written and in writing	section 5(6)

Transitional provisions

84.—(1) The provisions of this Part do not apply to arbitral proceedings commenced before the date on which this Part comes into force.

(2) They apply to arbitral proceedings commenced on or after that date under an arbitration agreement whenever made.

(3) The above provisions have effect subject to any transitional provision made by an order under section 109(2) (power to include transitional provisions in commencement order).

PART II OTHER PROVISIONS RELATING TO ARBITRATION

DOMESTIC ARBITRATION AGREEMENTS

Modification of Part I in relation to domestic arbitration agreement

85.—(1) In the case of a domestic arbitration agreement the provisions of Part I are modified in accordance with the following sections.

(2) For this purpose a "domestic arbitration agreement" means an arbitration agreement to which none of the parties is—

(a) an individual who is a national of, or habitually resident in, a state other than the United Kingdom, or

(b) a body corporate which is incorporated in, or whose central control and management is exercised in, a state other than the United Kingdom,

and under which the seat of the arbitration (if the seat has been designated or determined) is in the United Kingdom.

(3) In subsection (2) "arbitration agreement" and "seat of the arbitration" have the same meaning as in Part I (see sections 3, 5(1) and 6).

Staying of legal proceedings

86.—(1) In section 9 (stay of legal proceedings), subsection (4) (stay unless the arbitration agreement is null and void, inoperative, or incapable of being performed) does not apply to a domestic arbitration agreement.

(2) On an application under that section in relation to a domestic arbitration agreement the court shall grant a stay unless satisfied—

(a) that the arbitration agreement is null and void, inoperative, or incapable of being performed, or

(b) that there are other sufficient grounds for not requiring the parties to abide by the arbitration agreement.

(3) The court may treat as a sufficient ground under subsection (2)(b) the fact that the applicant is or was at any material time not ready and willing to do all things necessary for the proper conduct of the arbitration or of any other dispute resolution procedures required to be exhausted before resorting to arbitration.

(4) For the purposes of this section the question whether an arbitration agreement is a domestic arbitration agreement shall be determined by reference to the facts at the time the legal proceedings are commenced.

Effectiveness of agreement to exclude court's jurisdiction

87.—(1) In the case of a domestic arbitration agreement any agreement to exclude the jurisdiction of the court under—

(a) section 45 (determination of preliminary point of law), or

(b) section 69 (challenging the award: appeal on point of law),

is not effective unless entered into after the commencement of the arbitral proceedings in which the question arises or the award is made.

(2) For this purpose the commencement of the arbitral proceedings has the same meaning as in Part I (see section 14).

(3) For the purposes of this section the question whether an arbitration agreement is a domestic arbitration agreement shall be determined by reference to the facts at the time the agreement is entered into.

Power to repeal or amend sections 85 to 87

88.—(1) The Secretary of State may by order repeal or amend the provisions of sections 85 to 87.

(2) An order under this section may contain such supplementary, incidental and transitional provisions as appear to the Secretary of State to be appropriate.

(3) An order under this section shall be made by statutory instrument and no such order shall be made unless a draft of it has been laid before and approved by a resolution of each House of Parliament.

CONSUMER ARBITRATION AGREEMENTS

Application of unfair terms regulations to consumer arbitration agreements

89.—(1) The following sections extend the application of the Unfair Terms in Consumer Contracts Regulations 1994 in relation to a term which constitutes an arbitration agreement.

For this purpose "arbitration agreement" means an agreement to submit to arbitration present or future disputes or differences (whether or not contractual).

(2) In those sections "the Regulations" mean those regulations and includes any regulations amending or replacing those regulations.

(3) Those sections apply whatever the law applicable to the arbitration agreement.

Regulations apply where consumer is a legal person

90. The Regulations apply where the consumer is a legal person as they apply where the consumer is a natural person.

Arbitration agreement unfair where modest amount sought

91.—(1) A term which constitutes an arbitration agreement is unfair for the purposes of the Regulations so far as it relates to a claim for a pecuniary remedy which does not exceed the amount specified by order for the purposes of this section.

(2) Orders under this section may make different provision for different cases and for different purposes.

(3) The power to make orders under this section is exercisable—

(a) for England and Wales, by the Secretary of State with the concurrence of the Lord Chancellor,

(b) for Scotland, by the Secretary of State with the concurrence of the Lord Advocate, and
(c) for Northern Ireland, by the Department of Economic Development for Northern Ireland with the concurrence of the Lord Chancellor.

(4) Any such order for England and Wales or Scotland shall be made by statutory instrument which shall be subject to annulment in pursuance of a resolution of either House of Parliament.

(5) Any such order for Northern Ireland shall be a statutory rule for the purposes of the Statutory Rules (Northern Ireland) Order 1979 and shall be subject to negative resolution, within the meaning of section 41(6) of the Interpretation Act (Northern Ireland) Order 1954.

SMALL CLAIMS ARBITRATION IN THE COUNTY COURT

Exclusion of Part I in relation to small claims arbitration in the county court

92. Nothing in Part I of this Act applies to arbitration under section 64 of the County Courts Act 1984.

APPOINTMENT OF JUDGES AS ARBITRATORS

Appointment of judges as arbitrators

93.—(1) A judge of the Commercial Court or an official referee may, if in all the circumstances he thinks fit, accept appointment as a sole arbitrator or as umpire by or by virtue of an arbitration agreement.

(2) A judge of the Commercial Court shall not do so unless the Lord Chief Justice has informed him that, having regard to the state of business in the High Court and the Crown Court, he can be made available.

(3) An official referee shall not do so unless the Lord Chief Justice has informed him that, having regard to the state of official referees' business, he can be made available.

(4) The fees payable for the services of a judge of the Commercial Court or official referee as arbitrator or umpire shall be taken in the High Court.

(5) In this section—

"arbitration agreement" has the same meaning as in Part I and "official referee" means a person nominated under section

68(1)(a) of the Supreme Court Act 1981 to deal with official referees' business.

(6) The provisions of Part I of this Act apply to arbitration before a person appointed under this section with the modifications specified in Schedule 2.

STATUTORY ARBITRATIONS

Application of Part I to statutory arbitrations

94.—(1) The provisions of Part I apply to every arbitration under an enactment (a "statutory arbitration"), whether the enactment was passed or made before or after the commencement of this Act, subject to the adaptations and exclusions specified in sections 95 to 98.

(2) The provisions of Part I do not apply to a statutory arbitration if or to the extent that their application—

(a) is inconsistent with the provisions of the enactment concerned, with any rules or procedure authorised or recognised by it, or

(b) is excluded by any other enactment.

(3) In this section and the following provisions of this Part "enactment"—

(a) in England and Wales, includes an enactment contained in subordinate legislation within the meaning of the Interpretation Act 1978;

(b) in Northern Ireland, means a statutory provision within the meaning of section 1(f) of the Interpretation Act (Northern Ireland) 1954.

General adaptation of provisions in relation to statutory arbitrations

95.—(1) The provisions of Part I apply to a statutory arbitration—

(a) as if the arbitration were pursuant to an arbitration agreement and as if the enactment were that agreement, and

(b) as if the persons by and against whom a claim subject to arbitration in pursuance of the enactment may be or has been made were parties to that agreement.

(2) Every statutory arbitration shall be taken to have its seat in England and Wales or, as the case may be, in Northern Ireland.

Specific adaptations of provisions in relation to statutory arbitrations

96.—(1) The following provisions of Part I apply to a statutory arbitration with the following adaptations.

(2) In section 30(1) (competence of tribunal to rule on its own jurisdiction), the reference in paragraph (a) to whether there is a valid arbitration agreement shall be construed as a reference to whether the enactment applies to the dispute or difference in question.

(3) Section 35 (consolidation of proceedings and concurrent hearings) applies only so as to authorise the consolidation of proceedings, or concurrent hearings in proceedings, under the same enactment.

(4) Section 46 (rules applicable to substance of dispute) applies with the omission of subsection (1)(b) (determination in accordance with considerations agreed by parties).

Provisions excluded from applying to statutory arbitrations

97. The following provisions of Part I do not apply in relation to a statutory arbitration—

(a) section 8 (whether agreement discharged by death of a party);

(b) section 12 (power of court to extend agreed time limits);

(c) sections 9(5), 10(2) and 71(4) (restrictions on effect of provision that award condition precedent to right to bring legal proceedings).

Power to make further provision by regulations

98.—(1) The Secretary of State may make provision by regulations for adapting or excluding any provision of Part I in relation to statutory arbitrations in general or statutory arbitrations of any particular description.

(2) The power is exercisable whether the enactment concerned is passed or made before or after the commencement of this Act.

(3) Regulations under this section shall be made by statutory

instrument which shall be subject to annulment in pursuance of a resolution of either House of Parliament.

PART III RECOGNITION AND ENFORCEMENT OF CERTAIN FOREIGN AWARDS

ENFORCEMENT OF GENEVA CONVENTION AWARDS

Continuation of Part II of the Arbitration Act 1950

99. Part II of the Arbitration Act 1950 (enforcement of certain foreign awards) continues to apply in relation to foreign awards within the meaning of that Part which are not also New York Convention awards.

RECOGNITION AND ENFORCEMENT OF NEW YORK CONVENTION AWARDS

New York Convention awards

100.—(1) In this Part a "New York Convention award" means an award made, in pursuance of an arbitration agreement, in the territory of a state (other than the United Kingdom) which is a party to the New York Convention.

(2) For the purposes of subsection (1) and of the provisions of this Part relating to such awards—

(a) "arbitration agreement" means an arbitration agreement in writing, and

(b) an award shall be treated as made at the seat of the arbitration, regardless of where it was signed, despatched or delivered to any of the parties.

In this subsection "agreement in writing" and "seat of the arbitration" have the same meaning as in Part I.

(3) If Her Majesty by Order in Council declares that a state specified in the Order is a party to the New York Convention, or is a party in respect of any territory so specified, the Order shall, while in force, be conclusive evidence of that fact.

(4) In this section "the New York Convention" means the Convention on the Recognition and Enforcement of Foreign

Arbitral Awards adopted by the United Nations Conference on International Commercial Arbitration on 10th June 1958.

Recognition and enforcement of awards

101.—(1) A New York Convention award shall be recognised as binding on the persons as between whom it was made, and may accordingly be relied on by those persons by way of defence, set-off or otherwise in any legal proceedings in England and Wales or Northern Ireland.

(2) A New York Convention award may, by leave of the court, be enforced in the same manner as a judgment or order of the court to the same effect.

As to the meaning of "the court" see section 105.

(3) Where leave is so given, judgment may be entered in terms of the award.

Evidence to be produced by party seeking recognition or enforcement

102.—(1) A party seeking the recognition or enforcement of a New York Convention award must produce—

(a) the duly authenticated original award or a duly certified copy of it, and

(b) the original arbitration agreement or a duly certified copy of it.

(2) If the award or agreement is in a foreign language, the party must also produce a translation of it certified by an official or sworn translator or by a diplomatic or consular agent.

Refusal of recognition or enforcement

103.—(1) Recognition or enforcement of a New York Convention award shall not be refused except in the following cases.

(2) Recognition or enforcement of the award may be refused if the person against whom it is invoked proves—

(a) that a party to the arbitration agreement was (under the law applicable to him) under some incapacity;

(b) that the arbitration agreement was not valid under the law to which the parties subjected it or, failing any indication thereon, under the law of the country where the award was made;

(c) that he was not given proper notice of the appointment of the arbitrator or of the arbitration proceedings or was otherwise unable to present his case;

(d) that the award deals with a difference not contemplated by or not falling within the terms of the submission to arbitration or contains decisions on matters beyond the scope of the submission to arbitration (but see subsection (4));

(e) that the composition of the arbitral tribunal or the arbitral procedure was not in accordance with the agreement of the parties or, failing such agreement, with the law of the country in which the arbitration took place;

(f) that the award has not yet become binding on the parties, or has been set aside or suspended by a competent authority of the country in which, or under the law of which, it was made.

(3) Recognition or enforcement of the award may also be refused if the award is in respect of a matter which is not capable of settlement by arbitration, or if it would be contrary to public policy to recognise or enforce the award.

(4) An award which contains decisions on matters not submitted to arbitration may be recognised or enforced to the extent that it contains decisions on matters submitted to arbitration which can be separated from those on matters not so submitted.

(5) Where an application for the setting aside or suspension of the award has been made to such a competent authority as is mentioned in subsection (2)(f), the court before which the award is sought to be relied upon may, if it considers it proper, adjourn the decision on the recognition or enforcement of the award.

It may also on the application of the party claiming recognition or enforcement of the award order the other party to give suitable security.

Saving for other bases of recognition or enforcement

104. Nothing in the preceding provisions of this Part affects any right to rely upon or enforce a New York Convention award at common law or under section 66.

PART IV GENERAL PROVISIONS

Meaning of "the court": jurisdiction of High Court and county court

105.—(1) In this Act "the court" means the High Court or a county court, subject to the following provisions.

(2) The Lord Chancellor may by order make provision—

(a) allocating proceedings under this Act to the High Court or to county courts; or

(b) specifying proceedings under this Act which may be commenced or taken only in the High Court or in a county court.

(3) The Lord Chancellor may by order make provision requiring proceedings of any specified description under this Act in relation to which a county court has jurisdiction to be commenced or taken in one or more specified county courts.

Any jurisdiction so exercisable by a specified county court is exercisable throughout England and Wales or, as the case may be, Northern Ireland.

(4) An order under this section—

(a) may differentiate between categories of proceedings by reference to such criteria as the Lord Chancellor sees fit to specify, and

(b) may make such incidental or transitional provision as the Lord Chancellor considers necessary or expedient.

(5) An order under this section for England and Wales shall be made by statutory instrument which shall be subject to annulment in pursuance of a resolution of either House of Parliament.

(6) An order under this section for Northern Ireland shall be a statutory rule for the purposes of the Statutory Rules (Northern Ireland) Order 1979 which shall be subject to annulment in pursuance of a resolution of either House of Parliament in like manner as a statutory instrument and section 5 of the Statutory Instruments Act 1946 shall apply accordingly.

Crown application

106.—(1) Part I of this Act applies to any arbitration agreement to which Her Majesty, either in right of the Crown or of the Duchy of Lancaster or otherwise, or the Duke of Cornwall, is a party.

(2) Where Her Majesty is party to an arbitration agreement

otherwise than in right of the Crown, Her Majesty shall be represented for the purposes of any arbitral proceedings—

(a) where the agreement was entered into by Her Majesty in right of the Duchy of Lancaster, by the Chancellor of the Duchy or such person as he may appoint, and

(b) in any other case, by such person as Her Majesty may appoint in writing under the Royal Sign Manual.

(3) Where the Duke of Cornwall is party to an arbitration agreement, he shall be represented for the purposes of any arbitral proceedings by such person as he may appoint.

(4) References in Part I to a party or the parties to the arbitration agreement or to arbitral proceedings shall be construed, where subsection (2) or (3) applies, as references to the person representing Her Majesty or the Duke of Cornwall.

Consequential amendments and repeals

107.—(1) The enactments specified in Schedule 3 are amended in accordance with that Schedule, the amendments being consequential on the provisions of this Act.

(2) The enactments specified in Schedule 4 are repealed to the extent specified.

Extent

108.—(1) The provisions of this Act extend to England and Wales and, except as mentioned below, to Northern Ireland.

(2) The following provisions of Part II do not extend to Northern Ireland—

section 92 (exclusion of Part I in relation to small claims arbitration in the county court), and

section 93 and Schedule 2 (appointment of judges as arbitrators).

(3) Sections 89, 90 and 91 (consumer arbitration agreements) extend to Scotland and the provisions of Schedules 3 and 4 (consequential amendments and repeals) extend to Scotland as far as they relate to enactments which so extend, subject as follows.

(4) The repeal of the Arbitration Act 1975 extends only to England and Wales and Northern Ireland.

Commencement

109.—(1) The provisions of this Act come into force on such day as the Secretary of State may appoint by order made by statutory instrument, and different days may be appointed for different purposes.

(2) An order under subsection (1) may contain such transitional provisions as appear to the Secretary of State to be appropriate.

Short title

110. This Act may be cited as the Arbitration Act 1996.

SCHEDULE 1: MANDATORY PROVISIONS OF PART I (SECTION 4(1))

sections 9 to 11 (stay of legal proceedings);
section 12 (power of court to extend agreed time limits);
section 13 (application of Limitation Acts);
section 24 (power of court to remove arbitrator);
section 26(1) (effect of death of arbitrator);
section 28 (liability of parties for fees and expenses of arbitrators);
section 29 (immunity of arbitrator);
section 31 (objection to substantive jurisdiction of tribunal);
section 32 (determination of preliminary point of jurisdiction);
section 33 (general duty of tribunal);
section 37(2) (items to be treated as expenses of arbitrators);
section 40 (general duty of parties);
section 43 (securing the attendance of witnesses);
section 56 (power to withhold award in case of non-payment);
section 60 (effectiveness of agreement for payment of costs in any event);
section 66 (enforcement of award);
sections 67 and 68 (challenging the award: substantive jurisdiction and serious irregularity), and sections 70 and 71 (supplementary provisions; effect of order of court) so far as relating to those sections;
section 72 (saving for rights of person who takes no part in proceedings);
section 73 (loss of right to object);
section 74 (immunity of arbitral institutions, &c.);
section 75 (charge to secure payment of solicitors' costs).

SCHEDULE 2: MODIFICATIONS OF PART I IN RELATION TO JUDGE-ARBITRATORS (SECTION 93(6))

INTRODUCTORY

1. In this Schedule "judge-arbitrator" means a judge of the Commercial Court or official referee appointed as arbitrator or umpire under section 93.

GENERAL

2.—(1) Subject to the following provisions of this Schedule, references in Part I to the court shall be construed in relation to a judge-arbitrator, or in relation to the appointment of a judge-arbitrator, as references to the Court of Appeal.

(2) The references in sections 32(6), 45(6) and 69(8) to the Court of Appeal shall in such a case be construed as references to the House of Lords.

ARBITRATOR'S FEES

3.—(1) The power of the court in section 28(2) to order consideration and adjustment of the liability of a party for the fees of an arbitrator may be exercised by a judge-arbitrator.

(2) Any such exercise of the power is subject to the powers of the Court of Appeal under sections 24(4) and 25(3)(b) (directions as to entitlement to fees or expenses in case of removal or resignation).

EXERCISE OF COURT POWERS IN SUPPORT OF ARBITRATION

4.—(1) Where the arbitral tribunal consists of or includes a judge-arbitrator the powers of the court under sections 42 to 44 (enforcement of peremptory orders, summoning witnesses, and other court powers) are exercisable by the High Court and also by the judge-arbitrator himself.

(2) Anything done by a judge-arbitrator in the exercise of those powers shall be regarded as done by him in his capacity as judge of the High Court and have effect as if done by that court.

Nothing in this sub-paragraph prejudices any power vested in him as arbitrator or umpire.

EXTENSION OF TIME FOR MAKING AWARD

5.—(1) The power conferred by section 50 (extension of time for making award) is exercisable by the judge-arbitrator himself.

(2) Any appeal from a decision of a judge-arbitrator under that section lies to the Court of Appeal with the leave of that court.

WITHHOLDING AWARD IN CASE OF NON-PAYMENT

6.—(1) The provisions of paragraph 7 apply in place of the provisions of section 56 (power to withhold award in the case of non-payment) in relation to the withholding of an award for non-payment of the fees and expenses of a judge-arbitrator.

(2) This does not affect the application of section 56 in relation to the delivery of such an award by an arbitral or other institution or person vested by the parties with powers in relation to the delivery of the award.

7.—(1) A judge-arbitrator may refuse to deliver an award except upon payment of the fees and expenses mentioned in section 56(1).

(2) The judge-arbitrator may, on an application by a party to the arbitral proceedings, order that if he pays into the High Court the fees and expenses demanded, or such lesser amount as the judge-arbitrator may specify—

- (a) the award shall be delivered,
- (b) the amount of the fees and expenses properly payable shall be determined by such means and upon such terms as he may direct, and
- (c) out of the money paid into court there shall be paid out such fees and expenses as may be found to be properly payable and the balance of the money (if any) shall be paid out to the applicant.

(3) For this purpose the amount of fees and expenses properly payable is the amount the applicant is liable to pay under section 28 or any agreement relating to the payment of the arbitrator.

(4) No application to the judge-arbitrator under this paragraph may be made where there is any available arbitral process for appeal or review of the amount of the fees or expenses demanded.

(5) Any appeal from a decision of a judge-arbitrator under this paragraph lies to the Court of Appeal with the leave of that court.

(6) Where a party to arbitral proceedings appeals under sub-paragraph (5), an arbitrator is entitled to appear and be heard.

CORRECTION OF AWARD OR ADDITIONAL AWARD

8. Subsections (4) to (6) of section 57 (correction of award or additional award: time limit for application or exercise of power) do not apply to a judge-arbitrator.

COSTS

9. Where the arbitral tribunal consists of or includes a judge-arbitrator the powers of the court under section 63(4) (determination of recoverable costs) shall be exercised by the High Court.

10.—(1) The power of the court under section 64 to determine an arbitrator's reasonable fees and expenses may be exercised by a judge-arbitrator.

(2) Any such exercise of the power is subject to the powers of the Court of Appeal under sections 24(4) and 25(3)(b) (directions as to entitlement to fees or expenses in case of removal or resignation).

ENFORCEMENT OF AWARD

11. The leave of the court required by section 66 (enforcement of award) may in the case of an award of a judge-arbitrator be given by the judge-arbitrator himself.

SOLICITORS' COSTS

12. The powers of the court to make declarations and orders under the provisions applied by section 75 (power to charge property recovered in arbitral proceedings with the payment of solicitors' costs) may be exercised by the judge-arbitrator.

POWERS OF COURT IN RELATION TO SERVICE OF DOCUMENTS

13.—(1) The power of the court under section 77(2) (powers of court in relation to service of documents) is exercisable by the judge-arbitrator.

(2) Any appeal from a decision of a judge-arbitrator under that section lies to the Court of Appeal with the leave of that court.

POWERS OF COURT TO EXTEND TIME LIMITS RELATING TO ARBITRAL PROCEEDINGS

14.—(1) The power conferred by section 79 (power of court to extend time limits relating to arbitral proceedings) is exercisable by the judge-arbitrator himself.

(2) Any appeal from a decision of a judge-arbitrator under that section lies to the Court of Appeal with the leave of that court.

SCHEDULE 3: CONSEQUENTIAL AMENDMENTS (SECTION 107(1))

MERCHANT SHIPPING ACT 1894 (C. 60)

1. In section 496 of the Merchant Shipping Act 1894 (provisions as to deposits by owners of goods), after subsection (4) insert—

> "(5) In subsection (3) the expression 'legal proceedings' includes arbitral proceedings and as respects England and Wales and Northern Ireland the provisions of section 14 of the Arbitration Act 1996 apply to determine when such proceedings are commenced.".

STANNARIES COURT (ABOLITION) ACT 1896 (C. 45)

2. In section 4(1) of the Stannaries Court (Abolition) Act 1896 (references of certain disputes to arbitration), for the words from

"tried before" to "any such reference" substitute "referred to arbitration before himself or before an arbitrator agreed on by the parties or an officer of the court".

TITHE ACT 1936 (C. 43)

3. In section 39(1) of the Tithe Act 1936 (proceedings of Tithe Redemption Commission)—

(a) for "the Arbitration Acts 1889 to 1934" substitute "Part I of the Arbitration Act 1996";

(b) for paragraph (e) substitute—

"(e) the making of an application to the court to determine a preliminary point of law and the bringing of an appeal to the court on a point of law;";

(c) for "the said Acts" substitute "Part I of the Arbitration Act 1996".

EDUCATION ACT 1944 (C. 31)

4. In section 75(2) of the Education Act 1944 (proceedings of Independent School Tribunals) for "the Arbitration Acts 1889 to 1934" substitute "Part I of the Arbitration Act 1996".

COMMONWEALTH TELEGRAPHS ACT 1949 (C. 39)

5. In section 8(2) of the Commonwealth Telegraphs Act 1949 (proceedings of referees under the Act) for "the Arbitration Acts 1889 to 1934, or the Arbitration Act (Northern Ireland) 1937," substitute "Part I of the Arbitration Act 1996".

LANDS TRIBUNAL ACT 1949 (C. 42)

6. In section 3 of the Lands Tribunal Act 1949 (proceedings before the Lands Tribunal)—

(a) in subsection (6)(c) (procedural rules: power to apply Arbitration Acts), and

(b) in subsection (8) (exclusion of Arbitration Acts except as applied by rules),

for "the Arbitration Acts 1889 to 1934" substitute "Part I of the Arbitration Act 1996".

WIRELESS TELEGRAPHY ACT 1949 (C. 54)

7. In the Wireless Telegraphy Act 1949, Schedule 2 (procedure of appeals tribunal), in paragraph 3(1)—

(a) for the words "the Arbitration Acts 1889 to 1934" substitute "Part I of the Arbitration Act 1996";
(b) after the word "Wales" insert "or Northern Ireland" and
(c) for "the said Acts" substitute "Part I of that Act".

PATENTS ACT 1949 (C. 87)

8. In section 67 of the Patents Act 1949 (proceedings as to infringement of pre-1978 patents referred to comptroller), for "The Arbitration Acts 1889 to 1934" substitute "Part I of the Arbitration Act 1996".

NATIONAL HEALTH SERVICE (AMENDMENT) ACT 1949 (C. 93)

9. In section 7(8) of the National Health Service (Amendment) Act 1949 (arbitration in relation to hardship arising from the National Health Service Act 1946 or the Act), for "the Arbitration Acts 1889 to 1934" substitute "Part I of the Arbitration Act 1996" and for "the said Acts" substitute "Part I of that Act".

ARBITRATION ACT 1950 (C. 27)

10. In section 36(1) of the Arbitration Act 1950 (effect of foreign awards enforceable under Part II of that Act) for "section 26 of this Act" substitute "section 66 of the Arbitration Act 1996".

INTERPRETATION ACT (NORTHERN IRELAND) 1954 (C. 33 (N. I.))

11. In section 46(2) of the Interpretation Act (Northern Ireland) 1954 (miscellaneous definitions), for the definition of "arbitrator" substitute—

" "arbitrator" has the same meaning as in Part I of the Arbitration Act 1996;".

AGRICULTURAL MARKETING ACT 1958 (C. 47)

12. In section 12(1) of the Agricultural Marketing Act 1958 (application of provisions of Arbitration Act 1950)—

(a) for the words from the beginning to "shall apply" substitute "Sections 45 and 69 of the Arbitration Act 1996 (which relate to the determination by the court of questions of law) and section 66 of that Act (enforcement of awards) apply"; and

(b) for "an arbitration" substitute "arbitral proceedings".

CARRIAGE BY AIR ACT 1961 (C. 27)

13.—(1) The Carriage by Air Act 1961 is amended as follows.

(2) In section 5(3) (time for bringing proceedings)—

(a) for "an arbitration" in the first place where it occurs substitute "arbitral proceedings" and

(b) for the words from "and subsections (3) and (4)" to the end substitute "and the provisions of section 14 of the Arbitration Act 1996 apply to determine when such proceedings are commenced.".

(3) In section 11(c) (application of section 5 to Scotland)—

(a) for "subsections (3) and (4)" substitute "the provisions of section 14 of the Arbitration Act 1996"; and

(b) for "an arbitration" substitute "arbitral proceedings".

FACTORIES ACT 1961 (C. 34)

14. In the Factories Act 1961, for section 171 (application of Arbitration Act 1950), substitute—

"**Application of the Arbitration Act 1996**

171. Part I of the Arbitration Act 1996 does not apply to proceedings under this Act except in so far as it may be applied by regulations made under this Act.".

CLERGY PENSIONS MEASURE 1961 (NO. 3)

15. In the Clergy Pensions Measure 1961, section 38(4) (determination of questions), for the words "The Arbitration Act 1950" substitute "Part I of the Arbitration Act 1996".

TRANSPORT ACT 1962 (C. 46)

16.—(1) The Transport Act 1962 is amended as follows.

(2) In section 74(6)(f) (proceedings before referees in pension

disputes), for the words “the Arbitration Act 1950” substitute “Part I of the Arbitration Act 1996”.

(3) In section 81(7) (proceedings before referees in compensation disputes), for the words “the Arbitration Act 1950” substitute “Part I of the Arbitration Act 1996”.

(4) In Schedule 7, Part IV (pensions), in paragraph 17(5) for the words “the Arbitration Act 1950” substitute “Part I of the Arbitration Act 1996”.

CORN RENTS ACT 1963 (C. 14)

17. In the Corn Rents Act 1963, section 1(5) (schemes for apportioning corn rents, &c.), for the words “the Arbitration Act 1950” substitute “Part I of the Arbitration Act 1996”.

PLANT VARIETIES AND SEEDS ACT 1964 (C. 14)

18. In section 10(6) of the Plant Varieties and Seeds Act 1964 (meaning of “arbitration agreement”), for “the meaning given by section 32 of the Arbitration Act 1950” substitute “the same meaning as in Part I of the Arbitration Act 1996”.

LANDS TRIBUNAL AND COMPENSATION ACT (NORTHERN IRELAND) 1964 (C. 29 (N.I.))

19. In section 9 of the Lands Tribunal and Compensation Act (Northern Ireland) 1964 (proceedings of Lands Tribunal), in subsection (3) (where Tribunal acts as arbitrator) for “the Arbitration Act (Northern Ireland) 1937” substitute “Part I of the Arbitration Act 1996”.

INDUSTRIAL AND PROVIDENT SOCIETIES ACT 1965 (C. 12)

20.—(1) Section 60 of the Industrial and Provident Societies Act 1965 is amended as follows.

(2) In subsection (8) (procedure for hearing disputes between society and member, &c.)—

(a) in paragraph (a) for “the Arbitration Act 1950” substitute “Part I of the Arbitration Act 1996”; and

(b) in paragraph (b) omit “by virtue of section 12 of the said Act of 1950”.

(3) For subsection (9) substitute—

“(9) The court or registrar to whom any dispute is referred

under subsections (2) to (7) may at the request of either party state a case on any question of law arising in the dispute for the opinion of the High Court or, as the case may be, the Court of Session.".

CARRIAGE OF GOODS BY ROAD ACT 1965 (C. 37)

21. In section 7(2) of the Carriage of Goods by Road Act 1965 (arbitrations: time at which deemed to commence), for paragraphs (a) and (b) substitute—

"(a) as respects England and Wales and Northern Ireland, the provisions of section 14(3) to (5) of the Arbitration Act 1996 (which determine the time at which an arbitration is commenced) apply;".

FACTORIES ACT (NORTHERN IRELAND) 1965 (C. 20 (N.I.))

22. In section 171 of the Factories Act (Northern Ireland) 1965 (application of Arbitration Act), for "The Arbitration Act (Northern Ireland) 1937" substitute "Part I of the Arbitration Act 1996".

COMMONWEALTH SECRETARIAT ACT 1966 (C. 10)

23. In section 1(3) of the Commonwealth Secretariat Act 1966 (contracts with Commonwealth Secretariat to be deemed to contain provision for arbitration), for "the Arbitration Act 1950 and the Arbitration Act (Northern Ireland) 1937" substitute "Part I of the Arbitration Act 1996".

ARBITRATION (INTERNATIONAL INVESTMENT DISPUTES) ACT 1966 (C. 41)

24. In the Arbitration (International Investment Disputes) Act 1966, for section 3 (application of Arbitration Act 1950 and other enactments) substitute—

"Application of provisions of Arbitration Act 1996

3.—(1) The Lord Chancellor may by order direct that any of the provisions contained in sections 36 and 38 to 44 of the Arbitration Act 1996 (provisions concerning the conduct of arbitral proceedings, &c.) shall apply to such proceedings pursuant to the Convention as are specified in the order with or without any modifications or exceptions specified in the order.

(2) Subject to subsection (1), the Arbitration Act 1996 shall not apply to proceedings pursuant to the Convention, but this subsection shall not be taken as affecting section 9 of that Act (stay of legal proceedings in respect of matter subject to arbitration).

(3) An order made under this section—

(a) may be varied or revoked by a subsequent order so made, and

(b) shall be contained in a statutory instrument.".

POULTRY IMPROVEMENT ACT (NORTHERN IRELAND) 1968 (C. 12 (N.I.))

25. In paragraph 10(4) of the Schedule to the Poultry Improvement Act (Northern Ireland) 1968 (reference of disputes), for "The Arbitration Act (Northern Ireland) 1937" substitute "Part I of the Arbitration Act 1996".

INDUSTRIAL AND PROVIDENT SOCIETIES ACT (NORTHERN IRELAND) 1969 (C. 24 (N.I.))

26.—(1) Section 69 of the Industrial and Provident Societies Act (Northern Ireland) 1969 (decision of disputes) is amended as follows.

(2) In subsection (7) (decision of disputes)—

(a) in the opening words, omit the words from "and without prejudice" to "1937";

(b) at the beginning of paragraph (a) insert "without prejudice to any powers exercisable by virtue of Part I of the Arbitration Act 1996,"; and

(c) in paragraph (b) omit "the registrar or" and "registrar or" and for the words from "as might have been granted by the High Court" to the end substitute "as might be granted by the registrar".

(3) For subsection (8) substitute—

"(8) The court or registrar to whom any dispute is referred under subsections (2) to (6) may at the request of either party state a case on any question of law arising in the dispute for the opinion of the High Court.".

HEALTH AND PERSONAL SOCIAL SERVICES (NORTHERN IRELAND) ORDER 1972 (N.I. 14)

27. In Article 105(6) of the Health and Personal Social Services (Northern Ireland) Order 1972 (arbitrations under the Order), for "the Arbitration Act (Northern Ireland) 1937" substitute "Part I of the Arbitration Act 1996".

CONSUMER CREDIT ACT 1974 (C. 39)

28.—(1) Section 146 of the Consumer Credit Act 1974 is amended as follows.

(2) In subsection (2) (solicitor engaged in contentious business), for "section 86(1) of the Solicitors Act 1957" substitute "section 87(1) of the Solicitors Act 1974".

(3) In subsection (4) (solicitor in Northern Ireland engaged in contentious business), for the words from "business done" to "Administration of Estates (Northern Ireland) Order 1979" substitute "contentious business (as defined in Article 3(2) of the Solicitors (Northern Ireland) Order 1976.".

FRIENDLY SOCIETIES ACT 1974 (C. 46)

29.—(1) The Friendly Societies Act 1974 is amended as follows.

(2) For section 78(1) (statement of case) substitute—

> "(1) Any arbitrator, arbiter or umpire to whom a dispute falling within section 76 above is referred under the rules of a registered society or branch may at the request of either party state a case on any question of law arising in the dispute for the opinion of the High Court or, as the case may be, the Court of Session.".

(3) In section 83(3) (procedure on objections to amalgamations &c. of friendly societies), for "the Arbitration Act 1950 or, in Northern Ireland, the Arbitration Act (Northern Ireland) 1937" substitute "Part I of the Arbitration Act 1996".

INDUSTRY ACT 1975 (C. 68)

30. In Schedule 3 to the Industry Act (arbitration of disputes relating to vesting and compensation orders), in paragraph 14 (application of certain provisions of Arbitration Acts)—

(a) for "the Arbitration Act 1950 or, in Northern Ireland, the Arbitration Act (Northern Ireland) 1937" substitute "Part I of the Arbitration Act 1996", and

(b) for "that Act" substitute "that Part".

INDUSTRIAL RELATIONS (NORTHERN IRELAND) ORDER 1976 (N.I. 16)

31. In Article 59(9) of the Industrial Relations (Northern Ireland) Order 1976 (proceedings of industrial tribunal), for "The Arbitration Act (Northern Ireland) 1937" substitute "Part I of the Arbitration Act 1996".

AIRCRAFT AND SHIPBUILDING INDUSTRIES ACT 1977 (C. 3)

32. In Schedule 7 to the Aircraft and Shipbuilding Industries Act 1977 (procedure of Arbitration Tribunal), in paragraph 2—

(a) for "the Arbitration Act 1950 or, in Northern Ireland, the Arbitration Act (Northern Ireland) 1937" substitute "Part I of the Arbitration Act 1996", and

(b) for "that Act" substitute "that Part".

PATENTS ACT 1977 (C. 37)

33. In section 130 of the Patents Act 1977 (interpretation), in subsection (8) (exclusion of Arbitration Act) for "The Arbitration Act 1950" substitute "Part I of the Arbitration Act 1996".

JUDICATURE (NORTHERN IRELAND) ACT 1978 (C. 23)

34.—(1) The Judicature (Northern Ireland) Act 1978 is amended as follows.

(2) In section 35(2) (restrictions on appeals to the Court of Appeal), after paragraph (f) insert—

"(fa) except as provided by Part I of the Arbitration Act 1996, from any decision of the High Court under that Part;".

(3) In section 55(2) (rules of court), after paragraph (c) insert—

"(cc) providing for any prescribed part of the jurisdiction of the High Court in relation to the trial of any action involving matters of account to be exercised in the prescribed manner by a person agreed by the parties and for the remuneration of any such person;".

HEALTH AND SAFETY AT WORK (NORTHERN IRELAND) ORDER 1978 (N.I. 9)

35. In Schedule 4 to the Health and Safety at Work (Northern Ireland) Order 1978 (licensing provisions), in paragraph 3, for "The Arbitration Act (Northern Ireland) 1937" substitute "Part I of the Arbitration Act 1996".

COUNTY COURTS (NORTHERN IRELAND) ORDER 1980 (N.I. 3)

36.—(1) The County Courts (Northern Ireland) Order 1980 is amended as follows.

(2) In Article 30 (civil jurisdiction exercisable by district judge)—

(a) for paragraph (2) substitute—

"(2) Any order, decision or determination made by a district judge under this Article (other than one made in dealing with a claim by way of arbitration under paragraph (3)) shall be embodied in a decree which for all purposes (including the right of appeal under Part VI) shall have the like effect as a decree pronounced by a county court judge.";

(b) for paragraphs (4) and (5) substitute—

"(4) Where in any action to which paragraph (1) applies the claim is dealt with by way of arbitration under paragraph (3)—

(a) any award made by the district judge in dealing with the claim shall be embodied in a decree which for all purposes (except the right of appeal under Part VI) shall have the like effect as a decree pronounced by a county court judge;

(b) the district judge may, and shall if so required by the High Court, state for the determination of the High Court any question of law arising out of an award so made;

(c) except as provided by sub-paragraph (b), any award so made shall be final; and

(d) except as otherwise provided by county court rules, no costs shall be awarded in connection with the action.

(5) Subject to paragraph (4), county court rules may—

(a) apply any of the provisions of Part I of the Arbitration Act 1996 to arbitrations under paragraph (3) with such modifications as may be prescribed;

(b) prescribe the rules of evidence to be followed on any arbitration under paragraph (3) and, in particular, make provision with respect to the manner of taking and questioning evidence.

(5A) Except as provided by virtue of paragraph (5)(a), Part I of the Arbitration Act 1996 shall not apply to an arbitration under paragraph (3).".

(3) After Article 61 insert—

"APPEALS FROM DECISIONS UNDER PART I OF ARBITRATION ACT 1996

61A.—(1) Article 61 does not apply to a decision of a county court judge made in the exercise of the jurisdiction conferred by Part I of the Arbitration Act 1996.

(2) Any party dissatisfied with a decision of the county court made in the exercise of the jurisdiction conferred by any of the following provisions of Part I of the Arbitration Act 1996, namely—

(a) section 32 (question as to substantive jurisdiction of arbitral tribunal);
(b) section 45 (question of law arising in course of arbitral proceedings);
(c) section 67 (challenging award of arbitral tribunal: substantive jurisdiction);
(d) section 68 (challenging award of arbitral tribunal: serious irregularity);
(e) section 69 (appeal on point of law),

may, subject to the provisions of that Part, appeal from that decision to the Court of Appeal.

(3) Any party dissatisfied with any decision of a county court made in the exercise of the jurisdiction conferred by any other provision of Part I of the Arbitration Act 1996 may, subject to the provisions of that Part, appeal from that decision to the High Court.

(4) The decision of the Court of Appeal on an appeal under paragraph (2) shall be final.".

SUPREME COURT ACT 1981 (C. 54)

37.—(1) The Supreme Court Act 1981 is amended as follows.

(2) In section 18(1) (restrictions on appeals to the Court of Appeal), for paragraph (g) substitute—

"(g) except as provided by Part I of the Arbitration Act 1996, from any decision of the High Court under that Part;".

(3) In section 151 (interpretation, &c.), in the definition of "arbitration agreement", for "the Arbitration Act 1950 by virtue of section 32 of that Act;" substitute "Part I of the Arbitration Act 1996;".

MERCHANT SHIPPING (LINER CONFERENCES) ACT 1982 (C. 37)

38. In section 7(5) of the Merchant Shipping (Liner Conferences) Act 1982 (stay of legal proceedings), for the words from "section 4(1)" to the end substitute "section 9 of the Arbitration Act 1996 (which also provides for the staying of legal proceedings).".

AGRICULTURAL MARKETING (NORTHERN IRELAND) ORDER 1982 (N.I. 12)

39. In Article 14 of the Agricultural Marketing (Northern Ireland) Order 1982 (application of provisions of Arbitration Act (Northern Ireland) 1937)—

(a) for the words from the beginning to "shall apply" substitute "Section 45 and 69 of the Arbitration Act 1996 (which relate to the determination by the court of questions of law) and section 66 of that Act (enforcement of awards) apply"; and

(b) for "an arbitration" substitute "arbitral proceedings".

MENTAL HEALTH ACT 1983 (C. 20)

40. In section 78 of the Mental Health Act 1983 (procedure of Mental Health Review Tribunals), in subsection (9) for "The Arbitration Act 1950" substitute "Part I of the Arbitration Act 1996".

REGISTERED HOMES ACT 1984 (C. 23)

41. In section 43 of the Registered Homes Act 1984 (procedure of Registered Homes Tribunals), in subsection (3) for "The Arbitration Act 1950" substitute "Part I of the Arbitration Act 1996".

HOUSING ACT 1985 (C. 68)

42. In section 47(3) of the Housing Act 1985 (agreement as to determination of matters relating to service charges) for "section 32 of the Arbitration Act 1950" substitute "Part I of the Arbitration Act 1996".

LANDLORD AND TENANT ACT 1985 (C. 70)

43. In section 19(3) of the Landlord and Tenant Act 1985 (agreement as to determination of matters relating to service charges), for "section 32 of the Arbitration Act 1950" substitute "Part I of the Arbitration Act 1996".

CREDIT UNIONS (NORTHERN IRELAND) ORDER 1985 (N.I. 12)

44.—(1) Article 72 of the Credit Unions (Northern Ireland) Order 1985 (decision of disputes) is amended as follows.

(2) In paragraph (7)—

- (a) in the opening words, omit the words from "and without prejudice" to "1937";
- (b) at the beginning of sub-paragraph (a) insert "without prejudice to any powers exercisable by virtue of Part I of the Arbitration Act 1996,"; and
- (c) in sub-paragraph (b) omit "the registrar or" and "registrar or" and for the words from "as might have been granted by the High Court" to the end substitute "as might be granted by the registrar".

(3) For paragraph (8) substitute—

"(8) The court or registrar to whom any dispute is referred under paragraphs (2) to (6) may at the request of either party state a case on any question of law arising in the dispute for the opinion of the High Court.".

AGRICULTURAL HOLDINGS ACT 1986 (C. 5)

45. In section 84(1) of the Agricultural Holdings Act 1986 (provisions relating to arbitration), for "the Arbitration Act 1950" substitute "Part I of the Arbitration Act 1996".

INSOLVENCY ACT 1986 (C. 45)

46. In the Insolvency Act 1986, after section 349 insert—

"Arbitration agreements to which bankrupt is party

349A.—(1) This section applies where a bankrupt had become party to a contract containing an arbitration agreement before the commencement of his bankruptcy.

(2) If the trustee in bankruptcy adopts the contract, the arbitration agreement is enforceable by or against the trustee in relation to matters arising from or connected with the contract.

(3) If the trustee in bankruptcy does not adopt the contract and a matter to which the arbitration agreement applies requires to be determined in connection with or for the purposes of the bankruptcy proceedings—

(a) the trustee with the consent of the creditors' committee, or

(b) any other party to the agreement,

may apply to the court which may, if it thinks fit in all the circumstances of the case, order that the matter be referred to arbitration in accordance with the arbitration agreement.

(4) In this section—

"arbitration agreement" has the same meaning as in Part I of the Arbitration Act 1996 and

"the court" means the court which has jurisdiction in the bankruptcy proceedings.".

BUILDING SOCIETIES ACT 1986 (C. 53)

47. In Part II of Schedule 14 to the Building Societies Act 1986 (settlement of disputes: arbitration), in paragraph 5(6) for "the Arbitration Act 1950 and the Arbitration Act 1979 or, in Northern Ireland, the Arbitration Act (Northern Ireland) 1937" substitute "Part I of the Arbitration Act 1996".

MENTAL HEALTH (NORTHERN IRELAND) ORDER 1986 (N.I. 4)

48. In Article 83 of the Mental Health (Northern Ireland) Order 1986 (procedure of Mental Health Review Tribunal), in paragraph (8) for "The Arbitration Act (Northern Ireland) 1937" substitute "Part I of the Arbitration Act 1996".

MULTILATERAL INVESTMENT GUARANTEE AGENCY ACT 1988 (C. 8)

49. For section 6 of the Multilateral Investment Guarantee Agency Act 1988 (application of Arbitration Act) substitute—

"Application of Arbitration Act

6.—(1) The Lord Chancellor may by order made by statutory instrument direct that any of the provisions of sections 36 and 38 to 44 of the Arbitration Act 1996 (provisions in relation to the conduct of the arbitral proceedings, &c.) apply, with such modifications or exceptions as are specified in the order, to such arbitration proceedings pursuant to Annex II to the Convention as are specified in the order.

(2) Except as provided by an order under subsection (1) above, no provision of Part I of the Arbitration Act 1996 other than section 9 (stay of legal proceedings) applies to any such proceedings.".

COPYRIGHT, DESIGNS AND PATENTS ACT 1988 (C. 48)

50. In section 150 of the Copyright, Designs and Patents Act 1988 (Lord Chancellor's power to make rules for Copyright Tribunal), for subsection (2) substitute—

"(2) The rules may apply in relation to the Tribunal, as respects proceedings in England and Wales or Northern Ireland, any of the provisions of Part I of the Arbitration Act 1996.".

FAIR EMPLOYMENT (NORTHERN IRELAND) ACT 1989 (C. 32)

51. In the Fair Employment (Northern Ireland) Act 1989, section 5(7) (procedure of Fair Employment Tribunal), for "The Arbitration Act (Northern Ireland) 1937" substitute "Part I of the Arbitration Act 1996".

LIMITATION (NORTHERN IRELAND) ORDER 1989 (N.I. 11)

52. In Article 2(2) of the Limitation (Northern Ireland) Order 1989 (interpretation), in the definition of "arbitration agreement",

for "the Arbitration Act (Northern Ireland) 1937" substitute "Part I of the Arbitration Act 1996".

INSOLVENCY (NORTHERN IRELAND) ORDER 1989 (N.I. 19)

53. In the Insolvency (Northern Ireland) Order 1989, after Article 320 insert—

"Arbitration agreements to which bankrupt is party

320A.—(1) This Article applies where a bankrupt had become party to a contract containing an arbitration agreement before the commencement of his bankruptcy.

(2) If the trustee in bankruptcy adopts the contract, the arbitration agreement is enforceable by or against the trustee in relation to matters arising from or connected with the contract.

(3) If the trustee in bankruptcy does not adopt the contract and a matter to which the arbitration agreement applies requires to be determined in connection with or for the purposes of the bankruptcy proceedings—

(a) the trustee with the consent of the creditors' committee, or

(b) any other party to the agreement,

may apply to the court which may, if it thinks fit in all the circumstances of the case, order that the matter be referred to arbitration in accordance with the arbitration agreement.

(4) In this Article—

"arbitration agreement" has the same meaning as in Part I of the Arbitration Act 1996; and

"the court" means the court which has jurisdiction in the bankruptcy proceedings.".

SOCIAL SECURITY ADMINISTRATION ACT 1992 (C. 5)

54. In section 59 of the Social Security Administration Act 1992 (procedure for inquiries, &c.), in subsection (7), for "The Arbitration Act 1950" substitute "Part I of the Arbitration Act 1996".

SOCIAL SECURITY ADMINISTRATION (NORTHERN IRELAND) ACT 1992 (C. 8)

55. In section 57 of the Social Security Administration (Northern Ireland) Act 1992 (procedure for inquiries, &c.), in subsection (6)

for "the Arbitration Act (Northern Ireland) 1937" substitute "Part I of the Arbitration Act 1996".

TRADE UNION AND LABOUR RELATIONS (CONSOLIDATION) ACT 1992 (C. 52)

56. In sections 212(5) and 263(6) of the Trade Union and Labour Relations (Consolidation) Act 1992 (application of Arbitration Act) for "the Arbitration Act 1950" substitute "Part I of the Arbitration Act 1996".

INDUSTRIAL RELATIONS (NORTHERN IRELAND) ORDER 1992 (N.I. 5)

57. In Articles 84(9) and 92(5) of the Industrial Relations (Northern Ireland) Order 1992 (application of Arbitration Act) for "The Arbitration Act (Northern Ireland) 1937" substitute "Part I of the Arbitration Act 1996".

REGISTERED HOMES (NORTHERN IRELAND) ORDER 1992 (N.I. 20)

58. In Article 33(3) of the Registered Homes (Northern Ireland) Order 1992 (procedure of Registered Homes Tribunal) for "The Arbitration Act (Northern Ireland) 1937" substitute "Part I of the Arbitration Act 1996".

EDUCATION ACT 1993 (C. 35)

59. In section 180(4) of the Education Act 1993 (procedure of Special Educational Needs Tribunal), for "The Arbitration Act 1950" substitute "Part I of the Arbitration Act 1996".

ROADS (NORTHERN IRELAND) ORDER 1993 (N.I. 15)

60.—(1) The Roads (Northern Ireland) Order 1993 is amended as follows.

(2) In Article 131 (application of Arbitration Act) for "the Arbitration Act (Northern Ireland) 1937" substitute "Part I of the Arbitration Act 1996".

(3) In Schedule 4 (disputes), in paragraph 3(2) for "the Arbitration Act (Northern Ireland) 1937" substitute "Part I of the Arbitration Act 1996".

MERCHANT SHIPPING 1995 (C. 21)

61. In Part II of Schedule 6 to the Merchant Shipping Act 1995 (provisions having effect in connection with Convention Relating to the Carriage of Passengers and Their Luggage by Sea), for paragraph 7 substitute—

"7. Article 16 shall apply to arbitral proceedings as it applies to an action and, as respects England and Wales and Northern Ireland, the provisions of section 14 of the Arbitration Act 1996 apply to determine for the purposes of that Article when an arbitration is commenced.".

INDUSTRIAL TRIBUNALS ACT 1996 (C. 17)

62. In section 6(2) of the Industrial Tribunals Act 1996 (procedure of industrial tribunals), for "The Arbitration Act 1950" substitute "Part I of the Arbitration Act 1996".

SCHEDULE 4: REPEALS (SECTION 107(2))

Chapter	Short title	Extent of repeal
1892 c. 43.	Military Lands Act 1892.	In section 21(b), the words "under the Arbitration Act 1889".
1922 c. 51.	Allotments Act 1922.	In section 21(3), the words "under the Arbitration Act 1889".
1937 c. 8 (N.I.).	Arbitration Act (Northern Ireland) 1937.	The whole Act.
1949 c. 54.	Wireless Telegraphy Act 1949.	In Schedule 2, paragraph 3(3).
1949 c. 97.	National Parks and Access to the Countryside Act 1949.	In section 18(4), the words from "Without prejudice" to "England or Wales".

Chapter	Short title	Extent of repeal
1950 c. 27.	Arbitration Act 1950.	Part I. Section 42(3).
1958 c. 47.	Agricultural Marketing Act 1958.	Section 53(8).
1962 c. 46.	Transport Act 1962.	In Schedule 11, Part II, paragraph 7.
1964 c. 14.	Plant Varieties and Seeds Act 1964.	In section 10(4) the words from "or in section 9" to "three arbitrators)". Section 39(3)(b)(i).
1964 c. 29 (N.I.).	Lands Tribunal and Compensation Act (Northern Ireland) 1964.	In section 9(3) the words from "so, however, that" to the end.
1965 c. 12.	Industrial and Provident Societies Act 1965.	In section 60(8)(b), the words "by virtue of section 12 of the said Act of 1950".
1965 c. 37.	Carriage of Goods by Road Act 1965.	Section 7(2)(b).
1965 c. 13 (N.I.).	New Towns Act (Northern Ireland) 1965.	In section 27(2), the words from "under and in accordance with" to the end.
1969 c. 24 (N.I.).	Industrial and Provident Societies Act (Northern Ireland) 1969.	In section 69(7)— (a) in the opening words, the words from "and without prejudice" to "1937"; (b) in paragraph (b), the words "the registrar or" and "registrar or".

Chapter	Short title	Extent of repeal
1970 c. 31.	Administration of Justice Act 1970.	Section 4. Schedule 3.
1973 c. 41.	Fair Trading Act 1973.	Section 33(2)(d).
1973 N.I. 1.	Drainage (Northern Ireland) Order 1973.	In Article 15(4), the words from "under and in accordance" to the end. Article 40(4). In Schedule 7, in paragraph 9(2), the words from "under and in accordance" to the end.
1974 c. 47.	Solicitors Act 1974.	In section 87(1), in the definition of "contentious business", the words "appointed under the Arbitration Act 1950".
1975 c. 3.	Arbitration Act 1975.	The whole Act.
1975 c. 74.	Petroleum and Submarine Pipe-Lines Act 1975.	In Part II of Schedule 2— (a) in model clause 40(2), the words "in accordance with the Arbitration Act 1950"; (b) in model clause 40(2B), the words "in accordance with the Arbitration Act (Northern Ireland) 1937".

Chapter	Short title	Extent of repeal
		In Part II of Schedule 3, in model clause 38(2), the words "in accordance with the Arbitration Act 1950".
1976 N.I. 12.	Solicitors (Northern Ireland) Order 1976.	In Article 3(2), in the entry "contentious business", the words "appointed under the Arbitration Act (Northern Ireland) 1937".
		Article 71H(3).
1977 c. 37.	Patents Act 1977.	In section 52(4) the words "section 21 of the Arbitration Act 1950 or, as the case may be, section 22 of the Arbitration Act (Northern Ireland) 1937 (statement of cases by arbitrators); but".
		Section 131(e).
1977 c. 38.	Administration of Justice Act 1977.	Section 17(2).
1978 c. 23.	Judicature (Northern Ireland) Act 1978.	In section 35(2), paragraph (g)(v).
		In Schedule 5, the amendment to the Arbitration Act 1950.
1979 c. 42.	Arbitration Act 1979.	The whole Act.

Chapter	Short title	Extent of repeal
1980 c. 58.	Limitation Act 1980.	Section 34.
1980 N.I. 3.	County Courts (Northern Ireland) Order 1980.	Article 31(3).
1981 c. 54.	Supreme Court Act 1981.	Section 148.
1982 c. 27.	Civil Jurisdiction and Judgements Act 1982.	Section 25(3)(c) and (5). In section 26— (a) in subsection (1), the words "to arbitration or"; (b) in subsection (1)(a)(i), the words "arbitration or"; (c) in subsection (2), the words "arbitration or".
1982 c. 53.	Administration of Justice Act 1982.	Section 15(6). In Schedule 1, Part IV.
1984 c. 5.	Merchant Shipping Act 1984.	Section 4(8).
1984 c. 12.	Telecommunications Act 1984.	Schedule 2, paragraph 13(8).
1984 c. 16.	Foreign Limitation Periods Act 1984.	Section 5.
1984 c. 28.	County Courts Act 1984.	In Schedule 2, paragraph 70.
1985 c. 61.	Administration of Justice Act 1985.	Section 58. In Schedule 9, paragraph 15.
1985 c. 68.	Housing Act 1985.	In Schedule 18, in paragraph 6(2) the words from "and the Arbitration Act 1950" to the end.

Chapter	Short title	Extent of repeal
1985 N.I. 12.	Credit Unions (Northern Ireland) Order 1985.	In Article 72(7)— (a) in the opening words, the words from "and without prejudice" to "1937"; (b) in sub-paragraph (b), the words "the registrar or" and "registrar or".
1986 c. 45.	Insolvency Act 1986.	In Schedule 14, the entry relating to the Arbitration Act 1950.
1988 c. 8.	Multilateral Investment Guarantee Agency Act 1988.	Section 8(3).
1988 c. 21.	Consumer Arbitration Agreements Act 1988.	The whole Act.
1989 N.I. 11.	Limitation (Northern Ireland) Order 1989.	Article 72. In Schedule 3, paragraph 1.
1989 N.I. 19.	Insolvency (Northern Ireland) Order 1989.	In Part II of Schedule 9, paragraph 66.
1990 c. 41.	Courts and Legal Services Act 1990.	Sections 99 and 101 to 103.
1991 N.I. 7.	Food Safety (Northern Ireland) Order 1991.	In Articles 8(8) and 11(10), the words from "and the provisions" to the end.
1992 c. 40.	Friendly Societies Act 1992.	In Schedule 16, paragraph 30(1).

Chapter	Short title	Extent of repeal
1995 c. 8.	Agricultural Tenancies Act 1995.	Section 28(4).
1995 c. 21.	Merchant Shipping Act 1995.	Section 96(10). Section 264(9).
1995 c. 42.	Private International Law (Miscellaneous Provisions) Act 1995.	Section 3.

APPENDIX 3

THE UNCITRAL MODEL ARBITRATION RULES

General Assembly Resolution 31/98

UNCITRAL Arbitration Rules

Section I. Introductory rules

Scope of application (Article 1) and model
Arbitration clause
Notice, calculation of periods of time (Article 2)
Notice of arbitration (Article 3)
Representation and assistance (Article 4)

Section II. Composition of the arbitral tribunal

Number of arbitrators (Article 5)
Appointment of arbitrators (Articles 6 to 8)
Challenge of arbitrators (Articles 9 to 12)
Replacement of an arbitrator (Article 13)
Repetition of hearings in the event of the replacement of an arbitrator (Article 14)

Section III. Arbitral proceedings

General provisions (Article 15)
Place of arbitration (Article 16)
Language (Article 17)
Statement of claim (Article 18)
Statement of defence (Article 19)
Amendments to the claim or defence (Article 20)
Pleas as to the jurisdiction of the arbitral tribunal (Article 21)
Further written statements (Article 22)
Periods of time (Article 23)
Evidence and hearings (Articles 24 and 25)
Interim measures of protection (Article 26)

RESOLUTION 31/98 ADOPTED BY THE GENERAL ASSEMBLY ON 15 DECEMBER 1976

31/98. Arbitration Rules of the United Nations Commission on International Trade Law

The General Assembly,

Recognising the value of arbitration as a method of settling disputes arising in the context of international commercial relations,

Being convinced that the establishment of rules for ad hoc arbitration that are acceptable in countries with different legal, social and economic systems would significantly contribute to the development of harmonious international economic relations,

Bearing in mind that the Arbitration Rules of the United Nations Commission on International Trade Law have been prepared after extensive consultation with arbitral institutions and centres of international commercial arbitration,

Noting that the Arbitration Rules were adopted by the United Nations Commission on International Trade Law at its ninth session after due deliberation,

1. Recommends the use of the Arbitration Rules of the United Nations Commission on International Trade Law in the settlement of disputes arising in the context of international commercial relations, particularly by reference to the Arbitration Rules in commercial contracts;

2. Requests the Secretary-General to arrange for the widest possible distribution of the Arbitration Rules.

UNCITRAL ARBITRATION RULES

SECTION I. INTRODUCTORY RULES

Scope of application

Article 1

1. Where the parties to a contract have agreed in writing* that disputes in relation to that contract shall be referred to arbitration under the UNCITRAL Arbitration Rules, then such disputes shall be settled in accordance with these Rules subject to such modification as the parties may agree in writing.
2. These Rules shall govern the arbitration except that where any of these Rules is in conflict with a provision of the law applicable to the arbitration from which the parties cannot derogate, that provision shall prevail.

Notice, calculation of periods of time

Article 2

1. For the purposes of these Rules, any notice, including a notification, communication or proposal, is deemed to have been received if it is physically delivered to the addressee or if it is delivered at his habitual residence, place of business or mailing address, or, if none of these can be found after making reasonable inquiry, then at the addressees last known residence or place of business. Notice shall be deemed to have been received on the day it is so delivered.
2. For the purposes of calculating a period of time under these Rules, such period shall begin to run on the day following the day when a notice, notification, communication or proposal is received. If the last day of such period is an official holiday or a non-business day at the residence or place of business of the addressee, the period is extended until the first business day which follows. Official holidays

* MODEL ARBITRATION CLAUSE

Any dispute, controversy or claim arising out of or relating to this contract, or the breach, termination or invalidity thereof, shall be settled by arbitration in accordance with the UNCITRAL Arbitration Rules as at present in force.

Note—Parties may wish to consider adding:

(a) The appointing authority shall be . . . (name of institution or person);
(b) The number of arbitrators shall be . . . (one or three);
(c) The place of arbitration shall be . . . (town or country);
(d) The language(s) to be used in the arbitral proceedings shall be . . .

or nonbusiness days occurring during the running of the period of time are included in calculating the period.

Notice of arbitration

Article 3

1. The party initiating recourse to arbitration (hereinafter called the "claimant") shall give to the other party (hereinafter called the respondent) a notice of arbitration.
2. Arbitral proceedings shall be deemed to commence on the date on which the notice of arbitration is received by the respondent.
3. The notice of arbitration shall include the following:

- *(a)* A demand that the dispute be referred to arbitration;
- *(b)* The names and addresses of the parties;
- *(c)* A reference to the arbitration clause or the separate arbitration agreement that is invoked;
- *(d)* A reference to the contract out of or in relation to which the dispute arises;
- *(e)* The general nature of the claim and an indication of the amount involved, if any;
- *(f)* The relief or remedy sought;
- *(g)* A proposal as to the number of arbitrators (i.e. one or three), if the parties have not previously agreed thereon.

4. The notice of arbitration may also include:

- *(a)* The proposals for the appointments of a sole arbitrator and an appointing authority referred to in article 6, paragraph 1;
- *(b)* The notification of the appointment of an arbitrator referred to in article 7;
- *(c)* The statement of claim referred to in article 18.

Representation and assistance

Article 4

The parties may be represented or assisted by persons of their choice. The names and addresses of such persons must be communicated in writing to the other party; such communication must specify whether the appointment is being made for purposes of representation or assistance.

SECTION II. COMPOSITION OF THE ARBITRAL TRIBUNAL

Number of arbitrators

Article 5

If the parties have not previously agreed on the number of arbitrators (i.e. one or three), and if within 15 days after the receipt by the respondent of the notice of arbitration the parties have not agreed that there shall be only one arbitrator, three arbitrators shall be appointed.

Appointment of arbitrators (Articles 6 to 8)

Article 6

1. If a sole arbitrator is to be appointed, either party may propose to the other:

   (a) The names of one or more persons, one of whom would serve as the sole arbitrator; and

   (b) If no appointing authority has been agreed upon by the parties, the name or names of one or more institutions or persons, one of whom would serve as appointing authority.

2. If within 30 days after receipt by a party of a proposal made in accordance with paragraph 1 the parties have not reached agreement on the choice of a sole arbitrator, the sole arbitrator shall be appointed by the appointing authority agreed upon by the parties. If no appointing authority has been agreed upon by the parties, or if the appointing authority agreed upon refuses to act or fails to appoint the arbitrator within 60 days of the receipt of a party's request therefor, either party may request the Secretary-General of the Permanent Court of Arbitration at The Hague to designate an appointing authority.

3. The appointing authority shall, at the request of one of the parties, appoint the sole arbitrator as promptly as possible. In making the appointment the appointing authority shall use the following list-procedure, unless both parties agree that the list procedure should not be used or unless the appointing authority determines in its discretion that the use of the list-procedure is not appropriate for the case:

(a) At the request of one of the parties the appointing authority shall communicate to both parties an identical list containing at least three names;
(b) Within 15 days after the receipt of his list, each party may return the list to the appointing authority after having deleted the name or names to which he objects and numbered the remaining names on the list in the order of his preference;
(c) After the expiration of the above period of time the appointing authority shall appoint the sole arbitrator from among the names approved on the lists returned to it and in accordance with the order of preference indicated by the parties;
(d) If for any reason the appointment cannot be made according to this procedure, the appointing authority may exercise its discretion in appointing the sole arbitrator.

4. In making the appointment, the appointing authority shall have regard to such considerations as are likely to secure the appointment of an independent and impartial arbitrator and shall take into account as well the advisability of appointing an arbitrator of a nationality other than the nationalities of the parties.

Article 7

1. If three arbitrators are to be appointed, each party shall appoint one arbitrator. The two arbitrators thus appointed shall choose the third arbitrator who will act as the presiding arbitrator of the tribunal.

2. If within 30 days after the receipt of a party's notification of the appointment of an arbitrator the other party has not notified the first party of the arbitrator he has appointed:

(a) The first party may request the appointing authority previously designated by the parties to appoint the second arbitrator; or
(b) If no such authority has been previously designated by the parties, or if the appointing authority previously designated refuses to act or fails to appoint the arbitrator within 30 days after receipt of a party's request therefor, the first party may request the Secretary-General of the Permanent Court of Arbitration at The Hague to designate the appointing authority. The first party may then request the

appointing authority so designated to appoint the second arbitrator. In either case, the appointing authority may exercise its discretion in appointing the arbitrator.

3. If within 30 days after the appointment of the second arbitrator the two arbitrators have not agreed on the choice of the presiding arbitrator, the presiding arbitrator shall be appointed by an appointing authority in the same way as a sole arbitrator would be appointed under article 6.

Article 8

1. When an appointing authority is requested to appoint an arbitrator pursuant to article 6 or article 7, the party which makes the request shall send to the appointing authority a copy of the notice of arbitration, a copy of the contract out of or in relation to which the dispute has arisen and a copy of the arbitration agreement if it is not contained in the contract. The appointing authority may require from either party such information as it deems necessary to fulfil its function.

2. Where the names of one or more persons are proposed for appointment as arbitrators, their full names, addresses and nationalities shall be indicated, together with a description of their qualifications.

Challenge of arbitrators (Articles 9 to 12)

Article 9

A prospective arbitrator shall disclose to those who approach him in connexion with his possible appointment any circumstances likely to give rise to justifiable doubts as to his impartiality or independence. An arbitrator, once appointed or chosen, shall disclose such circumstances to the parties unless they have already been informed by him of these circumstances.

Article 10

1. Any arbitrator may be challenged if circumstances exist that give rise to justifiable doubts as to the arbitrators impartiality or independence.

2. A party may challenge the arbitrator appointed by him only for

reasons of which he becomes aware after the appointment has been made.

Article 11

1. A party who intends to challenge an arbitrator shall send notice of his challenge within 15 days after the appointment of the challenged arbitrator has been notified to the challenging party or within 15 days after the circumstances mentioned in articles 9 and 10 became known to that party.
2. The challenge shall be notified to the other party, to the arbitrator who is challenged and to the other members of the arbitral tribunal. The notification shall be in writing and shall state the reasons for the challenge.
3. When an arbitrator has been challenged by one party, the other party may agree to the challenge. The arbitrator may also, after the challenge, withdraw from his office. In neither case does this imply acceptance of the validity of the grounds for the challenge. In both cases the procedure provided in article 6 or 7 shall be used in full for the appointment of the substitute arbitrator, even if during the process of appointing the challenged arbitrator a party had failed to exercise his right to appoint or to participate in the appointment.

Article 12

1. If the other party does not agree to the challenge and the challenged arbitrator does not withdraw, the decision on the challenge will be made:

(a) When the initial appointment was made by an appointing authority, by that authority;

(b) When the initial appointment was not made by an appointing authority, but an appointing authority has been previously designated, by that authority;

(c) In all other cases, by the appointing authority to be designated in accordance with the procedure for designating an appointing authority as provided for in article 6.

2. If the appointing authority sustains the challenge, a substitute arbitrator shall be appointed or chosen pursuant to the procedure applicable to the appointment or choice of an arbitrator as provided in articles 6 to 9 except that, when this procedure would call for the designation of an appointing authority, the appointment of the

arbitrator shall be made by the appointing authority which decided on the challenge.

Replacement of an arbitrator

Article 13

1. In the event of the death or resignation of an arbitrator during the course of the arbitral proceedings, a substitute arbitrator shall be appointed or chosen pursuant to the procedure provided for in articles 6 to 9 that was applicable to the appointment or choice of the arbitrator being replaced.
2. In the event that an arbitrator fails to act or in the event of the *de jure* or *de facto* impossibility of his performing his functions, the procedure in respect of the challenge and replacement of an arbitrator as provided in the preceding articles shall apply.

Repetition of hearings in the event of the replacement of an arbitrator

Article 14

If under articles 11 to 13 the sole or presiding arbitrator is replaced, any hearings held previously shall be repeated; if any other arbitrator is replaced, such prior hearings may be repeated at the discretion of the arbitral tribunal.

SECTION III. ARBITRAL PROCEEDINGS

General provisions

Article 15

1. Subject to these Rules, the arbitral tribunal may conduct the arbitration in such manner as it considers appropriate, provided that the parties are treated with equality and that at any stage of the proceedings each party is given a full opportunity of presenting his case.
2. If either party so requests at any stage of the proceedings, the arbitral tribunal shall hold hearings for the presentation of evidence by witnesses, including expert witnesses, or for oral argument. In the absence of such a request, the arbitral tribunal shall decide whether

to hold such hearings or whether the proceedings shall be conducted on the basis of documents and other materials.
3. All documents or information supplied to the arbitral tribunal by one party shall at the same time be communicated by that party to the other party.

Place of arbitration

Article 16

1. Unless the parties have agreed upon the place where the arbitration is to be held, such place shall be determined by the arbitral tribunal, having regard to the circumstances of the arbitration.
2. The arbitral tribunal may determine the locale of the arbitration within the country agreed upon by the parties. It may hear witnesses and hold meetings for consultation among its members at any place it deems appropriate, having regard to the circumstances of the arbitration.
3. The arbitral tribunal may meet at any place it deems appropriate for the inspection of goods, other property or documents. The parties shall be given sufficient notice to enable them to be present at such inspection.
4. The award shall be made at the place of arbitration.

Language

Article 17

1. Subject to an agreement by the parties, the arbitral tribunal shall, promptly after its appointment, determine the language or languages to be used in the proceedings. This determination shall apply to the statement of claim, the statement of defence, and any further written statements and, if oral hearings take place, to the language or languages to be used in such hearings.
2. The arbitral tribunal may order that any documents annexed to the statement of claim or statement of defence, and any supplementary documents or exhibits submitted in the course of the proceedings, delivered in their original language, shall be accompanied by a translation into the language or languages agreed upon by the parties or determined by the arbitral tribunal.

Statement of claim

Article 18

1. Unless the statement of claim was contained in the notice of arbitration, within a period of time to be determined by the arbitral tribunal, the claimant shall communicate his statement of claim in writing to the respondent and to each of the arbitrators. A copy of the contract, and of the arbitration agreement if not contained in the contract, shall be annexed thereto.
2. The statement of claim shall include the following particulars:
   (a) The names and addresses of the parties;
   (b) A statement of the facts supporting the claim;
   (c) The points at issue;
   (d) The relief or remedy sought.

The claimant may annex to his statement of claim all documents he deems relevant or may add a reference to the documents or other evidence he will submit.

Statement of defence

Article 19

1. Within a period of time to be determined by the arbitral tribunal, the respondent shall communicate his statement of defence in writing to the claimant and to each of the arbitrators.
2. The statement of defence shall reply to the particulars *(b)*, *(c)* and *(d)* of the statement of claim (article 18, para. 2). The respondent may annex to his statement the documents on which he relies for his defence or may add a reference to the documents or other evidence he will submit.
3. In his statement of defence, or at a later stage in the arbitral proceedings if the arbitral tribunal decides that the delay was justified under the circumstances the respondent may make a counter-claim arising out of the same contract or rely on a claim arising out of the same contract for the purpose of a set-off.
4. The provisions of article 18, paragraph 2, shall apply to a counter-claim and a claim relied on for the purpose of a set-off.

Amendments to the claim or defence

Article 20

During the course of the arbitral proceedings either party may amend or supplement his claim or defence unless the arbitral tribunal considers it inappropriate to allow such amendment having regard to the delay in making it or prejudice to the other party or any other circumstances. However, a claim may not be amended in such a manner that the amended claim falls outside the scope of the arbitration clause or separate arbitration agreement.

Pleas as to the jurisdiction of the arbitral tribunal

Article 21

1. The arbitral tribunal shall have the power to rule on objections that it has no jurisdiction, including any objections with respect to the existence or validity of the arbitration clause or of the separate arbitration agreement.
2. The arbitral tribunal shall have the power to determine the existence or the validity of the contract of which an arbitration clause forms a part. For the purposes of article 21, an arbitration clause which forms part of a contract and which provides for arbitration under these Rules shall be treated as an agreement independent of the other terms of the contract. A decision by the arbitral tribunal that the contract is null and void shall not entail *ipso jure* the invalidity of the arbitration clause.
3. A plea that the arbitral tribunal does not have jurisdiction shall be raised not later than in the statement of defence or, with respect to a counter-claim, in the reply to the counter-claim.
4. In general, the arbitral tribunal should rule on a plea concerning its jurisdiction as a preliminary question. However, the arbitral tribunal may proceed with the arbitration and rule on such a plea in their final award.

Further written statements

Article 22

The arbitral tribunal shall decide which further written statements, in addition to the statement of claim and the statement of defence, shall be required from the parties or may be presented by them and shall fix the periods of time for communicating such statements.

Periods of time

Article 23

The periods of time fixed by the arbitral tribunal for the communication of written statements (including the statement of claim and statement of defence) should not exceed 45 days. However, the arbitral tribunal may extend the time-limits if it concludes that an extension is justified.

Evidence and hearings (Articles 24 and 25)

Article 24

1. Each party shall have the burden of proving the facts relied on to support his claim or defence.
2. The arbitral tribunal may, if it considers it appropriate, require a party to deliver to the tribunal and to the other party, within such a period of time as the arbitral tribunal shall decide, a summary of the documents and other evidence which that party intends to present in support of the facts in issue set out in his statement of claim or statement of defence.
3. At any time during the arbitral proceedings the arbitral tribunal may require the parties to produce documents, exhibits or other evidence within such a period of time as the tribunal shall determine.

Article 25

1. In the event of an oral hearing, the arbitral tribunal shall give the parties adequate advance notice of the date, time and place thereof.
2. If witnesses are to be heard, at least 15 days before the hearing each party shall communicate to the arbitral tribunal and to the other party the names and addresses of the witnesses he intends to present, the subject upon and the languages in which such witnesses will give their testimony.
3. The arbitral tribunal shall make arrangements for the translation of oral statements made at a hearing and for a record of the hearing if either is deemed necessary by the tribunal under the circumstances of the case, or if the parties have agreed thereto and have

communicated such agreement to the tribunal at least 15 days before the hearing.
4. Hearings shall be held *in camera* unless the parties agree otherwise. The arbitral tribunal may require the retirement of any witness or witnesses during the testimony of other witnesses. The arbitral tribunal is free to determine the manner in which witnesses are examined.
5. Evidence of witnesses may also be presented in the form of written statements signed by them.
6. The arbitral tribunal shall determine the admissibility, relevance, materiality and weight of the evidence offered.

Interim measures of protection

Article 26

1. At the request of either party, the arbitral tribunal may take any interim measures it deems necessary in respect of the subject-matter of the dispute, including measures for the conservation of the goods forming the subject-matter in dispute, such as ordering their deposit with a third person or the sale of perishable goods.
2. Such interim measures may be established in the form of an interim award. The arbitral tribunal shall be entitled to require security for the costs of such measures.
3. A request for interim measures addressed by any party to a judicial authority shall not be deemed incompatible with the agreement to arbitrate, or as a waiver of that agreement.

Experts

Article 27

1. The arbitral tribunal may appoint one or more experts to report to it, in writing, on specific issues to be determined by the tribunal. A copy of the experts terms of reference, established by the arbitral tribunal, shall be communicated to the parties.
2. The parties shall give the expert any relevant information or produce for his inspection any relevant documents or goods that he may require of them. Any dispute between a party and such expert as to the relevance of the required information or production shall be referred to the arbitral tribunal for decision.
3. Upon receipt of the experts report, the arbitral tribunal shall

communicate a copy of the report to the parties who shall be given the opportunity to express, in writing, their opinion on the report. A party shall be entitled to examine any document on which the expert has relied in his report.

4. At the request of either party the expert, after delivery of the report, may be heard at a hearing where the parties shall have the opportunity to be present and to interrogate the expert. At this hearing either party may present expert witnesses in order to testify on the points at issue. The provisions of article 25 shall be applicable to such proceedings.

Default

Article 28

1. If, within the period of time fixed by the arbitral tribunal, the claimant has failed to communicate his claim without showing sufficient cause for such failure, the arbitral tribunal shall issue an order for the termination of the arbitral proceedings. If, within the period of time fixed by the arbitral tribunal, the respondent has failed to communicate his statement of defence without showing sufficient cause for such failure, the arbitral tribunal shall order that the proceedings continue.

2. If one of the parties, duly notified under these Rules, fails to appear at a hearing, without showing sufficient cause for such failure, the arbitral tribunal may proceed with the arbitration.

3. If one of the parties, duly invited to produce documentary evidence, fails to do so within the established period of time, without showing sufficient cause for such failure, the arbitral tribunal may make the award on the evidence before it.

Closure of hearings

Article 29

1. The arbitral tribunal may inquire of the parties if they have any further proof to offer or witnesses to be heard or submissions to make and, if there are none, it may declare the hearings closed.

2. The arbitral tribunal may, if it considers it necessary owing to exceptional circumstances, decide, on its own motion or upon

application of a party, to reopen the hearings at any time before the award is made.

Waiver of rules

Article 30

A party who knows that any provision of, or requirement under, these Rules has not been complied with and yet proceeds with the arbitration without promptly stating his objection to such non-compliance, shall be deemed to have waived his right to object.

SECTION IV. THE AWARD

Decisions

Article 31

1. When there are three arbitrators, any award or other decision of the arbitral tribunal shall be made by a majority of the arbitrators.
2. In the case of questions of procedure, when there is no majority or when the arbitral tribunal so authorises, the presiding arbitrator may decide on his own, subject to revision, if any, by the arbitral tribunal.

Form and effect of the award

Article 32

1. In addition to making a final award, the arbitral tribunal shall be entitled to make interim, interlocutory, or partial awards.
2. The award shall be made in writing and shall be final and binding on the parties. The parties undertake to carry out the award without delay.
3. The arbitral tribunal shall state the reasons upon which the award is based, unless the parties have agreed that no reasons are to be given.
4. An award shall be signed by the arbitrators and it shall contain the date on which and the place where the award was made. Where there are three arbitrators and one of them fails to sign, the award shall state the reason for the absence of the signature.
5. The award may be made public only with the consent of both parties.
6. Copies of the award signed by the arbitrators shall be communicated to the parties by the arbitral tribunal.

7. If the arbitration law of the country where the award is made requires that the award be filed or registered by the arbitral tribunal, the tribunal shall comply with this requirement within the period of time required by law.

Applicable law, aimable compositeur

Article 33

1. The arbitral tribunal shall apply the law designated by the parties as applicable to the substance of the dispute. Failing such designation by the parties, the arbitral tribunal shall apply the law determined by the conflict of laws rules which it considers applicable.
2. The arbitral tribunal shall decide as *aimable compositeur* or *ex aequo et bono* only if the parties have expressly authorised the arbitral tribunal to do so and if the law applicable to the arbitral procedure permits such arbitration.
3. In all cases, the arbitral tribunal shall decide in accordance with the terms of the contract and shall take into account the usages of the trade applicable to the transaction.

Settlement or other grounds for termination

Article 34

1. If, before the award is made, the parties agree on a settlement of the dispute, the arbitral tribunal shall either issue an order for the termination of the arbitral proceedings or, if requested by both parties and accepted by the tribunal, record the settlement in the form of an arbitral award on agreed terms. The arbitral tribunal is not obliged to give reasons for such an award.
2. If, before the award is made, the continuation of the arbitral proceedings becomes unnecessary or impossible for any reason not mentioned in paragraph 1, the arbitral tribunal shall inform the parties of its intention to issue an order for the termination of the proceedings. The arbitral tribunal shall have the power to issue such an order unless a party raises justifiable grounds for objection.
3. Copies of the order for termination of the arbitral proceedings or of the arbitral award on agreed terms, signed by the arbitrators, shall

be communicated by the arbitral tribunal to the parties. Where an arbitral award on agreed terms is made, the provisions of article 32, paragraphs 2 and 4 to 7, shall apply.

Interpretation of the award

Article 35

1. Within 30 days after the receipt of the award, either party, with notice to the other party, may request that the arbitral tribunal give an interpretation of the award.
2. The interpretation shall be given in writing within 45 days after the receipt of the request. The interpretation shall form part of the award and the provisions of article 32, paragraphs 2 to 7, shall apply.

Correction of the award

Article 36

1. Within 30 days after the receipt of the award, either party, with notice to the other party, may request the arbitral tribunal to correct in the award any errors in computation, any clerical or typographical errors, or any errors of similar nature. The arbitral tribunal may within 30 days after the communication of the award make such corrections on its own initiative.
2. Such corrections shall be in writing, and the provisions of article 32, paragraphs 2 to 7, shall apply.

Additional award

Article 37

1. Within 30 days after the receipt of the award, either party, with notice to the other party, may request the arbitral tribunal to make an additional award as to claims presented in the arbitral proceedings but omitted from the award.
2. If the arbitral tribunal considers the request for an additional award to be justified and considers that the omission can be rectified without any further hearings or evidence, it shall complete its award within 60 days after the receipt of the request.
3. When an additional award is made, the provisions of article 32, paragraphs 2 to 7, shall apply.

Costs (Articles 38 to 40)

Article 38

The arbitral tribunal shall fix the costs of arbitration in its award. The term "costs" includes only:

(a) The fees of the arbitral tribunal to be stated separately as to each arbitrator and to be fixed by the tribunal itself in accordance with article 39;

(b) The travel and other expenses incurred by the arbitrators;

(c) The costs of expert advice and of other assistance required by the arbitral tribunal;

(d) The travel and other expenses of witnesses to the extent such expenses are approved by the arbitral tribunal;

(e) The costs for legal representation and assistance of the successful party if such costs were claimed during the arbitral proceedings, and only to the extent that the arbitral tribunal determines that the amount of such costs is reasonable;

(f) Any fees and expenses of the appointing authority as well as the expenses of the Secretary-General of the Permanent Court of Arbitration at The Hague.

Article 39

1. The fees of the arbitral tribunal shall be reasonable in amount, taking into account the amount in dispute, the complexity of the subject-matter, the time spent by the arbitrators and any other relevant circumstances of the case.
2. If an appointing authority has been agreed upon by the parties or designated by the Secretary-General of the Permanent Court of Arbitration at The Hague, and if that authority has issued a schedule of fees for arbitrators in international cases which it administers, the arbitral tribunal in fixing its fees shall take that schedule of fees into account to the extent that it considers appropriate in the circumstances of the case.
3. If such appointing authority has not issued a schedule of fees for arbitrators in international cases, any party may at any time request the appointing authority to furnish a statement setting forth the basis for establishing fees which is customarily followed in international cases in which the authority appoints arbitrators. If the appointing authority consents to provide such a statement, the arbitral tribunal

in fixing its fees shall take such information into account to the extent that it considers appropriate in the circumstances of the case.
4. In cases referred to in paragraphs 2 and 3, when a party so requests and the appointing authority consents to perform the function, the arbitral tribunal shall fix its fees only after consultation with the appointing authority which may make any comment it deems appropriate to the arbitral tribunal concerning the fees.

Article 40

1. Except as provided in paragraph 2, the costs of arbitration shall in principle be borne by the unsuccessful party. However, the arbitral tribunal may apportion each of such costs between the parties if it determines that apportionment is reasonable, taking into account the circumstances of the case.
2. With respect to the costs of legal representation and assistance referred to in article 38, paragraph *(e)*, the arbitral tribunal, taking into account the circumstances of the case, shall be free to determine which party shall bear such costs or may apportion such costs between the parties if it determines that apportionment is reasonable.
3. When the arbitral tribunal issues an order for the termination of the arbitral proceedings or makes an award on agreed terms, it shall fix the costs of arbitration referred to in article 38 and article 39, paragraph 1, in the text of that order or award.
4. No additional fees may be charged by an arbitral tribunal for interpretation or correction or completion of its award under articles 35 to 37.

Deposit of costs

Article 41

1. The arbitral tribunal, on its establishment, may request each party to deposit an equal amount as an advance for the costs referred to in article 38, paragraphs *(a)*, *(b)* and *(c)*.
2. During the course of the arbitral proceedings the arbitral tribunal may request supplementary deposits from the parties.
3. If an appointing authority has been agreed upon by the parties or designated by the Secretary-General of the Permanent Court of Arbitration at The Hague, and when a party so requests and the

appointing authority consents to perform the function, the arbitral tribunal shall fix the amounts of any deposits or supplementary deposits only after consultation with the appointing authority which may make any comments to the arbitral tribunal which it deems appropriate concerning the amount of such deposits and supplementary deposits.

4. If the required deposits are not paid in full within 30 days after the receipt of the request, the arbitral tribunal shall so inform the parties in order that one or another of them may make the required payment. If such payment is not made, the arbitral tribunal may order the suspension or termination of the arbitral proceedings.

5. After the award has been made, the arbitral tribunal shall render an accounting to the parties of the deposits received and return any unexpended balance to the parties.

GLOSSARY

Adjudication—The term applied to the decision given by a court or tribunal after it has considered the evidence put before it.

Arbitrator—The person appointed by or on behalf of the parties to consider the evidence of the parties and provide an award.

Award—The decision of the arbitrator which must be in writing and which is binding upon the parties provided the arbitrator was properly appointed.

Claimant—The person or body commencing an action in arbitral proceedings.

Court—The state body which will hear and adjudicate on the issues before it and which has the authority to impose sanctions on any member of the community for non-compliance with its orders, directions and adjudications. Some state tribunals have similar powers but they are usually restricted to a specified group of persons, e.g. employment tribunals.

Defendant—The person or body against whom legal proceedings are commenced.

Defence—The document in which the party serves its defence upon the plaintiff . This document will contain specific rebuttals or admissions to each allegation made by the plaintiff in the Statement of Claim (see also Points of Defence).

Mediator—A person appointed by the parties to help in the resolution of a dispute. He is described as neutral, meaning that he is totally independent of each and every party. He has no authority and his task is to help the parties come to a mutually acceptable settlement of the dispute.

Party—The term used to denote the person, group of people or body on one side of proceedings.

Plaintiff—The person or body commencing a legal action against another.

Pleadings—The term given to the documents issued by the parties in which they state their case and their response to the other side's case.

Points of Claim—The document in which the claimant sets out his case (see also Statement of Case).

Points of Defence—The term used in arbitrations for the defence.

Privilege—The term used to denote documents or other records which a party may not be forced to show to the other side in an action. This group will include a range of documents including communications between a lawyer and his client, documents which are privileged in the public interest and a number of other groups.

Reference—A word commonly used for the arbitration.

Respondent—The person or body against whom arbitral proceedings are commenced. It is also used to describe the defendant in certain other legal proceedings.

Specific Performance—This is the term applied to an Order which provides for the party to undertake a specific task such as repair a wall, dissolve a partnership, or other such non-monetary action.

Statement of Claim—The term used for the plaintiff's document in which he sets out his claim (see Points of Claim).

Statement of Case—The document in which a party to an arbitration sets out his case and which contains both the facts and law upon which he intends to rely.

Summons—The document by which the plaintiff commences an action in the county court. It is also used in a number of other legal contexts.

Subpoena—The document issued by the court requiring the attendance of a person at a trial or arbitration hearing.

Tribunal—The term applied to the person or persons who make up a "court" as in arbitral proceedings, and also in respect of various state bodies such as employment tribunals.

Without Prejudice—The term applied to negotiations between parties in dispute which refers to the fact that such negotiations are aimed at settling the issues between them. The basic rule is that nothing that is communicated between the parties in such circumstances can be used in any later court or tribunal action should the negotiations fail.

Writ—The document by which a party commences an action in the High Court.

INDEX